South Beach Diet Made Easy: Quick Start Guide

Aronas .G Mackie

All rights reserved. Copyright © 2023 Aronas .G Mackie

All rights reserved. Copyright © 2023 Aronas .G Mackie

Funny helpful tips:

Stay solution-focused; problems are inevitable, but solutions drive progress.

Learn the art of compromise; relationships thrive on mutual understanding and flexibility.

South Beach Diet Made Easy: Quick Start Guide : Effortlessly Achieve Your Health Goals with the Simplified South Beach Diet: A Beginner's Guide to Healthy Eating

Life advices:

Explore the world of digital currencies; cryptocurrencies and blockchain are reshaping the financial landscape.

Stay ethical in all business dealings; integrity builds trust and reputation.

Introduction

The South Beach Diet is a popular and effective diet plan designed to promote weight loss and improve overall health. This guide provides a comprehensive understanding of the South Beach Diet, its principles, guidelines, and recommended meal plans for different phases of the diet.

The guide begins by explaining the core concept of the South Beach Diet and the distinction between good and bad carbs. It emphasizes the importance of choosing the right carbohydrates to maintain stable blood sugar levels and support weight loss.

Next, the South Beach Diet guidelines are outlined, covering various food categories such as bread, breakfast cereals, dairy products, pasta, soups, fruits, and beverages. The guide educates readers on the types of foods that are suitable for each phase of the diet.

To delve deeper into the role of carbohydrates in the diet, a section is dedicated to explaining how carbs work and how the body responds to them. This information helps readers make informed choices about the foods they consume.

The guide offers meal plans tailored for each phase of the South Beach Diet. These meal plans provide detailed instructions on what to eat during Phase One, Phase Two, and Phase Three of the diet, making it easy for individuals to follow the diet and achieve their weight loss goals.

Additionally, the guide addresses the importance of exercise in conjunction with the South Beach Diet. It provides readers with daily challenges and workout routines that complement the diet program and promote a healthier lifestyle.

Common questions about the South Beach Diet and exercise program are addressed in the final section of the guide. These FAQs cover various aspects of the diet, helping readers gain clarity and confidence in following the South Beach Diet effectively.

Overall, this guide serves as a comprehensive resource for anyone interested in embarking on the South Beach Diet journey. It equips individuals with the knowledge and tools to make healthier food choices, achieve weight loss goals, and lead a more active and balanced lifestyle.

Contents

Chapter 1 – Understanding the South Beach Diet 1
   1. Phase One 1
   2. Phase Two...2
   3. Phase Three 3
   Good and Bad Carbs 3
Chapter 2 – The South Beach Diet Guidelines...6
   Breads 9
   Breakfast Cereals 10
   Dairy Food 10
   Pasta 10
   Soups 10
   Fruits...10
   Beverages 11
Chapter 3 – All About Carbohydrates 13
Chapter 4 – How Carbs Work and the Body'sResponse to Them 18
Chapter 5 – Meal Plans for Phase One of the South Beach Diet 22
   Day 1 22
   Day 2 26
   Day 3 29
   Day 4 33
   Day 5 36
   Day 6 39
   Day 7 42
Chapter 6 – Meal Plans for Phase Two of the South Beach Diet 47

Day 1 47
Day 2 50
Day 3 52
Day 4 55
Day 5 58
Day 6 60
Day 7 64
Chapter 7 – Meal Plans for Phase Three of the South Beach Diet 68
Day 1 68
Day 2 73
Day 3 77
Day 4 80
Day 5 84
Day 6 88
Day 7 92
Chapter 8 – The Daily Challenges and Workout Routines You Can Do 97
Chapter 9 – Common Questions about the South Beach Diet and Your Exercise Program 111

Chapter 1 – Understanding the South Beach Diet

If the South Beach Diet is not about low fat or low carb food, then what kind of diet does it advocate? The South Beach Diet teaches its followers the value of eating the right carbs and the right fats. These are the good ones that enable you to eat and enjoy food sans the presence of bad fats and bad carbs. As a result, you become healthier and lose weight — somewhere between 8 and 13 pounds in just two weeks. Now how's that as motivation?

This diet has existed for years, has helped a lot of overweight people succeed in their weight loss goals, and has helped in keeping the weight off for good.

There are three phases in the South Beach Diet:

1. Phase One

This is considered to be the most challenging and strictest part. During this phase, you are required to eat three balanced meals a day with two snacks (midmorning and midafternoon snacks). You are encouraged to eat plenty of vegetables, cheese, nuts, and eggs, and just normal-sized helpings of fish, chicken, meat, and shellfish. Salads are a must-eat particularly those sprinkled with organic olive oil. The most important thing is to drink plenty of water, although tea and coffee are allowed during this phase.

What makes the South Beach Diet different from other diets? Nothing, really! Except that for the next 14 days (Phase One), you will not be eating rice, potatoes, bread, or pasta. Not even fruit of any kind. Obviously, no sweets of any sort are allowed such as cakes, candies, chocolates, or ice cream. No alcoholic beverages are permitted, not even a drop.

Now here's the deal: you will begin adding those foods back into your diet after 2 weeks. Just go easy on the sweets! Or better yet, continue to avoid them completely.

What happens if cravings kick in? You will be surprised to find that within the first two weeks of this diet program, your cravings will disappear. The first three days may be challenging for beginners, but you will be amazed at how soon the days become weeks.

2. Phase Two

During this phase, you will already begin to see changes in your weight. Losing about 8 – 13 pounds in just two weeks is already an achievement, but this is just the beginning. After Phase 1, you will immediately notice that it is way easier to fit in that black dress as compared to before, and zipping up that pair of jeans suddenly becomes effortless. Those will be just some of the more noticeable changes.

Aside from this, you will notice that you have changed your attitude towards food. It is as if a switch has been turned on and you now see food not as a means to satisfy cravings but as the way to nourish the body. The physical cravings that once dominated your eating habits are now gone, and will stay that way for as long as you stick with the program.

You are losing weight not because you are eating less, but because you now eat less of the specific foods that created those bad cravings and urges in the first place. With this new dietary habit, you can expect to continue losing weight after Phase 2 ends even if you are gradually adding those forbidden foods back into your diet again. However, note that you are only allowed to pick one or two of these banished foods to reintroduce. If it is rice that you cannot live without, you can have it. If it is bread, you can reintroduce it to your diet. But you cannot have them all. That is the difference. Now, you get to enjoy them in a different way — a little less indulgently than before.

Phase Two will go on for as long as you are able to achieve your desired weight. It will depend on how much you want to lose. Those who are on Phase 2 are expected to lose weight at an average of a pound or two a week. As soon as you reach your target weight, it is time to move to the next phase.

3. Phase Three

This stage will last for as long as you live. When you have reached this phase, you will no longer feel as if you are on a speicial diet. Eating good carbs should be second nature to you. You now eat normal food served in normal-sized portions.

The phases basically teach you to become more aware of the kind of food to eat and their effects on your weight and health in general. They also alter your body's response to cravings.

Good and Bad Carbs

One side-effect of being overweight is that insulin's ability to process fats, sugar, and fuel is impaired. As a result, the body has no choice but to store more fats, particularly in the midsection.

What the body does is store more fats without burning them off. All these are due to the bad carbs that come from bread, rice, pasta, and other highly processed foods. According to studies, if you decrease the amount of bad carbs consumed in a day, your insulin resistance will begin to recover on its own.

There are two kinds of carbohydrates: sugars and starches. Sugars add flavor and calories. This is why it is recommended to eat them sparingly. Starches, on the other hand, also known as complex carbohydrates, are usually found in grains, potatoes, legumes, beans, and other vegetables.

When you gradually cut down your consumption of bad carbs, you will notice the following improvements in your body:

- your weight will begin a fairly rapid decrease
- your metabolism will rev up
- cravings slowly disappear
- lower blood sugar
- improved blood chemistry

This is the reason why the South Beach Diet promotes the consumption of good carbs (vegetables, fruits, and whole grains) and restricts the intake of bad carbs (highly processed food where all fiber has been stripped).

The South Beach Diet is not like other diet programs that totally eliminate carbohydrates in one's diet. If you cut carbohydrates for good, it would only permit saturated fats that could lead to different cardiovascular diseases. So even if you lose weight, your blood chemistry might suffer from eating too much saturated fat.

The plan is to cut certain carbohydrates, but not totally eliminate all of them. The good carbs are encouraged and the bad ones are discouraged. For example, if you banish white flour, you can still go for whole grains and whole wheat. Not everyone would want to give up those foods so this diet can still accommodate the desire to eat them, albiet not without restrictions.

The South Beach Diet permits the consumption of lean pork, lamb, meat, and beef. To compensate for the cut in carbohydrates, you are allowed to eat animal proteins. A strict restriction on meat, common in low-fat diets, is proven to be unnecessary as meat does not have a harmful effect on one's blood chemistry.

The following are some of the recommended foods in the South Beach Diet which would be prohibited in a low-fat diet:

- Egg yolks – good source of Vitamin E and promote balance between good and bad cholesterol

- Chicken
- Fish – mackerel, tuna, and salmon
- Nuts
- Yogurt
- Low-fat cheese
- Low-fat milk
- Oils – olive oil, canola, and peanut oil

Chapter 2 – The South Beach Diet Guidelines

Many diets fail primarily because they are too complicated and rigid. Most diet programs may be medically sound, but if they are difficult to follow, they will generally fail in practice. This is why the South Beach Diet is designed to be flexible and simple enough to follow only with few guidelines to take note of.

1. This diet allows dieters to eat the way they normally do. You will not be denied of every eating pleasure nor there be noticeable deprivation. The latter part of this book will provide menus and recipes to help you with your food plan.

2. This diet does not have complex menus and combinations. Because trying to find the right kind of food to eat on a daily basis is burdensome, many diets fail. Therefore, this diet is based on easy-to-make dishes with ingredients that can be easily found in the nearest grocery store.

3. This diet plan allows dieters to bend the rules provided that they know how to undo their deed. The good thing about the South Beach Diet is that the three-phase structure allows you to move easily from one stage to another. If for example you have overindulged in carbs or sweets during Phase 2, it would be easier to just switch back to Phase 1 and lose the excess weight, then return to where you have left off in Phase 2.

4. This diet is also known for the absence of complicated calorie counts, carbs, and fats. Portion sizes are not even an issue here. The major goal is to eat good carbs and good fats.

5. Although this diet acknowledges the importance of exercise in losing weight and keeping metabolism revved up, the South Beach Diet is not totally reliant on exercise alone. You will lose weight even if you don't exercise. However, you will shed even more pounds when you decide to combine this diet regimen with exercise. Therefore, it is still encouraged to get moving and stretch those muscles so it will be easier to melt those fats away and keep them off for good.

How does this diet go on a typical day?

The day before you begin Phase 1, you have probably eaten a good and memorable meal. By the time you wake up in the morning, your bloodstream is in a clean state. Your main goal is to keep it that way. This is possible if you start to eliminate the bad carbs.

To get started with Phase 1, you begin by preparing your first meal for the day. You can cook your usual fill of eggs either boiled or cooked in olive oil, and pair them with steamed asparagus or broccoli on the side. You may crave your usual morning bread, but if you can get your mind off it successfully, it will be easier to say no to other bad carbs. The first test is usually the hardest and this will determine if you can continue with this diet without your usual load of carbs.

During Phase 1, you must cut off all the carbs and go for healthier alternatives such as food high in fiber. Omit foods laden with sugar. This will be your diet for 2 weeks.

Surprisingly, you can pair this menu with coffee or tea. Some diets prohibit the intake of coffee as it intensifies cravings. But taking out coffee from the list would be excessively depriving for some people, as you have got enough modifications to contend with, without giving up your morning coffee too.

What is important is that you do not skip breakfast altogether. The problem with most dieters is that they are too busy to sit down and eat their breakfast or they just don't feel like eating in the morning. If you think you can save on calories by doing it this way, you are wrong. Skipping your first meal for the day would mean blood sugar dropping and your hunger increasing over the course of the morning. When this happens, you will surely overindulge come lunchtime and that will eventually show itself in a higher number on your bathroom scales. So if you are trying to lose weight, never skip breakfast.

On Meal Planning

When you have reached Phase 2, a meal plan will come in handy. You will notice in the next chapters that there are more dishes made with eggs. This diet makes liberal use of eggs because they contain good cholesterol with minimal saturated fats. As you go through Phase 2, some carbs will be reintroduced.

Come midmorning, you may feel the urge to eat. Do not just grab that bag of chips just yet. You would not want to break Phase 2. Instead, go for yogurt or cheese sticks. They are low in fat and do not add bad carbs apart from filling you up.

When the clock ticks lunchtime, you can opt for salad with varieties of greens and grilled fish or chicken. These dishes can easily be prepared at home. As for the portions; do not set limits. The goal of this diet is to satisfy your hunger so you will not crave unhealthy treats inbetween meals. Remember, portion sizes and calorie counts are absolutely not part of the South Beach Diet.

By now, you probably know by now how the diet goes as well as the pattern of meals. They are healthy combinations and are but normal fare. They are intended to satisfy your palate so you will not feel deprived of good food. The South Beach Diet is designed to be as simple as that. When you are taking in the right food (good carbs), you do not have to worry as to how much of these foods you eat. Protein and fats give you the feeling of being full much more than refined carbs.

It is likewise the goal of this diet for people to have a strong understanding of what kinds of food to eat without restraints, what kinds need to be eaten sparingly, and what kind to totally avoid. You will begin to understand the principles of blood chemistry and metabolism, and how they affect your weight. In fact, you will learn how to control them through your food choices. If you find yourself cheating a little today and a little more the next day, and you think you have broken the rules, it is easier to go back to square one.

To give you an idea, the following are the glycemic indexes of foods that you encounter every day. This will help you understand which types of food increase your blood sugar. In the South Beach Diet, you should particularly aim for food with a low Glycemic Index especially during Phase 1, and later on move to higher-GI foods once you have achieved your target weight loss.

Breads

Bran bread - GI: 68

Hamburger bun - GI: 87

Plain bagel - GI: 103

Gluten-free wheat bread - GI: 129

Cereal Grains

Rice - GI: 65

Brown rice - GI: 79

Couscous - GI: 93

Cornmeal - GI: 98

Breakfast Cereals

Oatmeal, noninstant - GI: 70

Kellog's Mini-wheats - GI: 81

Rice Krispies - GI: 117

Cornflakes - GI: 119

Dairy Food

Low fat yogurt - GI: 20

Whole milk - GI: 39

Fat-free milk - GI: 46

Ice cream - GI: 87

Pasta

Spaghetti - GI: 38

Fettuccine - GI: 46

Macaroni - GI: 64

Mac and cheese - GI: 92

Soups

Tomato soup - GI: 54

Lentil soup - GI: 63

Black bean soup - GI: 92

Green pea soup - GI: 94

Fruits

Apple - GI: 34

Orange - GI: 47
Grapes - GI: 62
Banana - GI: 89

Vegetables

Asparagus - GI: 20
Broccoli - GI: 20
Spinach - GI: 20
Tomatoes - GI: 20

Breads and Cakes

Sponge cake - GI: 66
Muffin - GI: 88
Croissant - GI: 96
Doughnuts - GI: 108

Cookies and Crackers

Oatmeal cookie - GI: 79
Biscotti - GI: 113
Wheat crackers - GI: 96
Rice cakes - GI: 110

Beverages

Soy milk - GI: 43
Juice (unsweetened) - GI: 57
Pineapple juice - GI: 66

Grapefruit juice - GI: 69

Once you have learned all these, it is easier to eat properly and stick to the diet plan.

Chapter 3 – All About Carbohydrates

By the time you have lasted through the two weeks of the first Phase, you are ready to start adding carbohydrates back into your diet again. At this point, the insulin resistance 'syndrome' has vanished. The cravings for sugar and other highly processed food are gone, too.

The challenge is to restrict dieters from immediately going for food with high glycemic index carbs after Phase 1. However, according to studies, dieters who are on a South Beach Diet and have managed to lose weight in the first 2 weeks were suddenly reluctant to eat the kind of food that made them overweight. So whether it is rice, pasta, or bread that made them fat, they totally avoid them as much as possible even if they are already on Phase 2. That is the effect of the South Beach Diet.

Still, there are valuable reasons to go back to having carbohydrates. The following are some of the carbs you can reintroduce come Phase 2:

1. Cereals – You can either eat these hot or cold. In the South Beach Diet, it is never encouraged to weigh your food, but if you are adding rice back into your menus, a serving no larger than a tennis ball is recommended.

2. Wholegrain bread – This can be eaten either during breakfast or dinner. Remember not to have bread for both breakfast and dinner.

3. Fruits – They are not carbohydrates but since they have been eliminated during Phase 1, it is now time to bring them back into action. It is usually recommended that you start with one piece of fruit a day. Apples and grapefruits are perfect examples since they have a low glycemic

index and won't cause a rise in your blood sugar. But be very careful eating fruits during breakfast. They provoke a big jolt of insulin and would trigger cravings when eaten in the morning.

The goal here is to add carbohydrates slowly but surely. If you added a piece of fruit a day with servings of bread or any other kind of carbs and you still kept on losing weight, then that is a good sign. But, if you have added too many fruits into your diet with other carbs and noticed that your weight is stuck, then it is time to cut back or try different carbs and monitor the results.

The most successful dieters of the South Beach Diet are those who are not afraid to try every recipe and see if it suits their tastes and preferences. They personalize the plan and take advantage of the variety of food that is permitted. Once they arrive at their weight loss goals, they stick to it and make it part of their lifestyle.

The major setback here is that some would get bored in the process and go back to their old eating habits. That is why it is important that you make the diet plan as diverse as possible. Look for substitutions and variations. The strategy of substitution can help you continue eating 'forbidden foods' provided that you substitute some ingredients with healthier alternatives. You just have to know which ingredients need replacement and be willing to try different food combinations.

The following are some of the best combos you can add to your culinary repertoire:

1. Peanut butter and jelly sandwich – This becomes less harmful because of the peanut butter. It contains monosaturated fat, resveratrol (the same beneficial protection you get from drinking red wine), and folate (helps in metabolizing homocysteine). Just take it easy on the jelly because it is similar to eating a bowl of sugar.

Your best bet would be all-natural peanut butter with a little bit of jelly. When it comes to bread, avoid the good old white bread. Instead, go for pita bread or wholewheat.

2. Bacon and egg – This is considered 'the' American breakfast. The South Beach Diet permits the consumption of egg given the nutrients it provides. The egg yields both good and bad carbohydrates, but the good thing is that it does not affect the ratio of the two. Bacon, on the other hand, is allowed only provided that you do not overindulge and you only go for the leaner one. As with the other breakfast staples such as bread and potatoes, it would be best to avoid them if you are trying to lose weight.

3. Banana Split and Orange Juice – Banana has a high glycemic index, up near mangoes and pineapples. So look for substitutes with lower glycemic index such as strawberries and blueberries. You can also munch on some nuts such as raw almonds, walnuts, and peanuts. Instead of the low-fat versions, it is suggested that you stick with the normal ones since most of these low-fat nuts only substitute fats with sugar – definitely not diet-friendly.

Understanding Food More

The equation behind obesity is plain simple: the faster sugars and starches are absorbed into the bloodstream, the quicker you get those bulges and see higher numbers on your bathroom scales. Succinctly, anything that speeds the process of digesting carbohydrates is not good and anything that slows it down is beneficial.

The good news is that you have the power to control the glycemic index of your food by choosing the ingredients and how you will prepare them. Take for instance the potato. You can make a lot of dishes with potato. What makes it fattening is what you do with it. This is the same as with your other favorite foods.

As much as possible, avoid baked food. The baking process makes the starches easily available to your digestive system. Did you know that even french fries are better than baked? This is because of the fat in which they are cooked.

The better alternatives to baked foods are boiled and mashed foods. Aside from the cooking process, you would eat them with only a small amount of butter or cream on top as compared to baked ones where you would add generous servings of butter and cream. But, not all baked goods are bad. You have to look at the ingredients. There are menus in this eBook that require baking, but notice that the ingredients are all healthy. This just goes to show you how some baked goods can have an effect on your South Beach Diet. So the next time you eat potatoes, be mindful of its varieties. It's better to go for white-skinned. The red-skinned version is the highest in carbs. If you can't help but indulge, eat sparingly.

Are White Breads Really Bad?

Yes. And it gets really bad if you are not a South Beach Dieter. It is better that you eat ice cream than choose the white version of bread. The former is less fattening.

So how do you choose your breads? The rule of thumb is to choose for the heavier and coarser versions. Whole and intact are better than sliced.

The following are other nutrients that slow down sugar absorption:

- Fiber – This is good because it delays the stomach's effort to get the sugars in carbohydrates. Even though fiber is not absorbed into the bloodstream, it still helps in digestion and in the normal functioning of your colon.

- Fats and proteins – These also slow the speed with which the stomach does its job on carbs. It's best to eat these when you eat carbs. For example, eating bread with some low-fat cheese is much better than eating the bread alone. Eating that baked potato with vegetables on the side is far better than munching on that baked potato alone.

Chapter 4 – How Carbs Work and the Body's Response to Them

As already stated in the previous chapters, carbohydrates are found in a varied array of food: everything from common vegetables to that sumptuous dessert. All carbohydrates contain sugars and they come in different forms – sucrose, lactose, maltose, and fructose. It is easy to tell which carbohydrates are sugar laden and which are not. Remember, the more sugar a food contains, the faster it is released. Simple math: faster sugar is worse, slower sugar is better.

When the sugars are absorbed slowly, your blood sugar rises gradually. The following slow and gradual decline in blood sugar makes for less cravings. This is the exact opposite if the sugar is absorbed at a much faster rate. The moment the pancreas detects a rapid rise in blood sugar, it immediately secretes high levels of insulin to deal with it. As a result, you have an immediate plunge in your blood sugar level. The blood sugar drops so low that your body begins to crave more carbs and sweets. Just to keep the body satisfied, you go beyond what is required for the day and gain more pounds in the process.

How are you going to stop this from happening? You have three strategies:

- First, eat food that causes only gradual increase in blood sugar.

- Second, prevent overeating and limit cravings by making sure that you have timely healthy snacks to hand.

- Third, there must be an understanding as to which foods cause the most rapid rise in blood sugar so you will not eat them when you get the chance.

Among the sugars discussed above, the highest and one that absorbs faster is maltose, the one found in beer. Now you know why there is such a thing as "beer belly". The immediate rise of blood sugar stimulates the rise in insulin production. This is why it is easier to accumulate fats around the midsection.

So what happens when you eat carbs?

Take for instance white bread. When you eat it, all you take in is carbs with no fiber. As a result, the bread is quickly transformed into glucose causing a rise in insulin. This leads to the rise and fall of your blood sugar level, which creates more cravings in the process. Eating white bread is similar to drinking beer on an empty stomach. You get nothing but sugar.

If your diet regularly consists of this, it is all the more important that you include fiber in your diet. Although it is not absorbed into the bloodstream, at least you get to excrete what you have consumed, through waste. The lack of fiber in one's diet is the main reason why you get constipated. This is needed in the diet so as not to get 'drunk on carbs'. And through the help of the South Beach Diet (eating the good carbs and eliminating the bad ones), you prevent hypoglycemia and control your weight.

Will I get diabetes if I don't change my lifestyle?

If you recognise yourself in the negative eating habits described so far in this chapter, you are a sure candidate for being diabetic. Most people know that it is through the body's inability to process sugar and starch properly that they become an easy target. As your body digests the food you eat, all the carbs are converted into glucose, or what you know as blood sugar. From there, it is the pancreas' job to detect the sudden rise in glucose. As a response, it produces insulin. This plays an important role in allowing major organs of the body to extract glucose from the bloodstream to either store or use it immediately.

Since the body is in need of constant supply of sugar for energy, the lack of it would make you feel dizzy or worse, go into coma. So, if sugars cannot enter and they remain lurking in the bloodstream, they're sure to cause harm to the body.

Another thing to clarify is that diabetes is not just about sugar. It is also the body's inability to properly process fats. Whenever you eat fats from meat and dairy products, it is also the job of insulin to transport these fatty acids from the bloodstream into the tissues in the body to be used for fuel or to store for future use.

One of the complications of obesity is diabetes. If you do not act on obesity and the body cannot properly transfer glucose and fatty acids from your bloodstream to the tissues, this could spell big trouble. Diabetes is surely on its way.

There are two types of diabetes:

1. Type 1 or Juvenile diabetes – This often occurs during childhood or adolescence. It is caused by damage in the pancreas resulting in the organ producing too little insulin to get the job done of getting sugar and fatty acids from the bloodstream. It is incurable, and at the moment, the only treatment is through daily insulin injections.

2. Type 2 diabetes – This is also known as the adult-onset diabetes. For this type, there is no virus to possibly blame. It is either genetic or lifestyle. Here, the pancreas is fully functional and is actually doing the opposite – producing too much insulin.

What has it got to do with the South Beach Diet?

A lot. When you carry excess fat in your body, it's difficult for the insulin to do its job. The blood sugar level will not be able to drop as quickly as it should thereby making the pancreas pump out more insulin to let the glucose in. Your pancreas then would overshoot the mark until your blood sugar comes to its low point. It is the rapid increase and immediate plunge that causes food cravings. This will result in you eating more carbs, and so the vicious cycle just goes on and on.

The above are the reasons why people overeat and why carbs make you hungrier. It also shows how these carbs could increase numbers on the scale that could later on develop into diabetes.

Could it also lead to heart disease?

Your being overweight is not mainly due to the number of fat cells in the body. In fact, the number of cells remain constant regardless of the weight you have. What happens to these cells is that they increase in size. Yes, these cells grow fat. And the moment they expand, the insulin will have difficulty unlocking them. This is why if you are overweight; the fat levels and sugar rise higher than normal.

When the insulin finds it difficult to open the lock, it takes longer to store the fat that you eat. Due to this delay, the liver becomes flooded with fatty acids. The organ then emits harmful molecules that deposit cholesterol and fat into the blood vessels of the heart. When this keep happening without you doing anything to stop it, blockage will soon occur. This is the link between obesity and heart disease.

The only cure for this is to change your lifestyle before it is too late. The South Beach Diet will help in more ways than one. Being physically fit not only means slimming down and being physically attractive, you will also have 'fit' blood vessels and healthy blood chemistry.

Chapter 5 – Meal Plans for Phase One of the South Beach Diet

Phase 1 is considered the strictest part of the plan, and lasts for two weeks. This is long enough to address the causes of insulin resistance — mainly, eating too many bad carbs.

During Phase 1, your meals do not have to necessarily be low carb, so long as you eat the right kind of carbs. This diet is designed to give allowances for ample portions of proteins, low glycemic index food, and good fats. Your menus should include low glycemic index vegetables, high fiber food, various protein-rich foods, and unlimited veggie salads.

By the time Phase 1 ends, you will notice a difference in how you view food. You will treat each day as an exciting opportunity to eat yet another good carb and a filling dish. Your cravings for sweets and highly-processed food will suddenly vanish and you no longer think of them as your comfort food. And because Phase 1 is the strictest of all phases, the servings are relatively small.

This program will let you eat 6 times in a day so you will not have to be craving food and feel deprived. Here is a meal plan with recipes for the next 7 days. Since Phase 1 lasts for 2 weeks, you may choose to repeat some of the recipes to complete the 2-week diet plan.

Day 1

Breakfast: Cheesy Veggies Frittata

Mid-morning snack: 1 cheese stick

Lunch: Salad with Grilled fish

Mid afternoon snack: 1 celery stick and low-fat cheese

Dinner: Chicken in Balsamic Vinegar
Dessert: Almond Ricotta

Breakfast

Cheesy Veggies Frittata

Ingredients:
- ½ tablespoon olive oil
- ½ cup onion, sliced
- ½ cup red bell pepper, sliced
- ½ cup zucchini, sliced
- ½ cup red bell pepper, sliced
- 2 plum tomatoes, diced
- 1 tablespoon basil
- Pinch of salt
- Pinch of pepper
- ½ cup liquid egg substitute
- 1.2 cup cottage cheese
- ¼ cup fat-free milk
- ¾ cup low-fat cheese, shredded

Directions:
1. In a skillet, heat the oil over medium heat. Add the onion, pepper, zucchini, and bell pepper. Saute for 3 minutes until all vegetables are lightly browned.

2. Add the tomatoes, basil, salt, and pepper. Cook for 3 minutes.

3. Meanwhile in a blender: Combine the egg substitute, cheese, and milk. Process for 3 minutes or until the mixture is smooth. Pour the mixture over the vegetables.

4. Cover and cook for 3 minutes or until it is set. Sprinkle with cheese.

Midmorning Snack – Cheese stick

Lunch

Salad with Grilled Fish

Ingredients:
- 5 leaves romaine lettuce, torn into bite-size pieces
- 1 tomato, chopped
- ½ cup red onion
- 1 cucumber, sliced
- ½ cup reduced-fat feta cheese
- 2 tablespoons extra virgin olive oil
- 1 teaspoon oregano leaves
- 2 tablespoons fresh lemon juice
- ½ teaspoon salt

Directions:
1. In a large bowl, combine the lettuce, tomatoes, onion, cucumber, and feta cheese.

2. Whisk together the oil, oregano, lemon juice, and salt. Pour the mixture and toss until coated.
3. Serve with grilled fish.

Mid afternoon snack: 1 celery stick and low-fat cheese

Dinner

Chicken in Balsamic Vinegar

Ingredients:
- 5 boneless chicken breast halves
- 2 cloves garlic, minced
- 1 teaspoon rosemary leaves, minced
- ½ teaspoon pepper
- ½ teaspoon salt
- 2 tablespoons extra virgin olive oil
- ¼ cup balsamic vinegar

Directions:
1. In a large bowl, combine the chicken, garlic, rosemary, and pepper. Drizzle with oil and spice mixture. Cover and marinade overnight.
2. Preheat the oven to 450 F. Spray the roasting pan with cooking spray and place the chicken on it. Bake for 10 minutes. Turn the chicken over and add water if the drippings begin to stick. Bake for another 10 minutes.
3. Drizzle the vinegar over the chicken and transfer to a plate. Serve.

Dessert

Almond Ricotta

Ingredients:

- ½ cup ricotta cheese
- ¼ teaspoon almond extract
- 1 package sugar substitute
- 1 teaspoon toasted almonds

Directions:

1. Mix the ricotta, almond extract, and sugar substitute in a bowl.
2. Refrigerate for 1 hour and serve.

Day 2

Breakfast: Mushrooms and Asparagus Omelet
Mid-morning snack: 1 wedge light cheese
Lunch: Crabmeat Salad with Greens
Midafternoon snack: Hummus with raw vegetables
Dinner: Grilled Salmon
Dessert: Ricotta Cheese in Lemon Zest

Breakfast

Mushrooms and Asparagus Omelet

Ingredients:

- 2 tablespoons water

- 3 stalks asparagus
- 2 eggs
- ¼ cup white mushrooms, sliced
- ¼ cup reduced-fat mozzarella cheese

Directions:

1. In a skillet, boil water. Once boiling, add the asparagus and cook, uncovered.
2. Meanwhile in a bowl, beat the eggs and water until completely blended.
3. Coat a skillet with olive oil and pour the egg mixture. Cook until the top begins to set. Fill one half of the omelet with asparagus, mushrooms, and cheese.
4. Fold the omelet and put on a serving plate. Serve.

Mid-morning snack: 1 wedge light cheese

Lunch

Crabmeat Salad with Greens

Ingredients:

- 2 cups watercress leaves
- 2 cups spinach
- 2 cups endive, torn
- 2 cups red leaf cabbage
- ½ cup red bell pepper
- ½ cup water chestnuts

- 12 oz crabmeat
- Mustard Sauce

Directions:

1. In a large bowl, combine the watercress leaves, spinach, endive, cabbage, bell pepper, and chestnuts. Toss well. Add the crabmeat.
2. Put some mustard sauce and serve.

Midafternoon snack: hummus with raw vegetables

Dinner

Grilled Salmon

Ingredients:

- 1 lb salmon
- 2 teaspoons extra virgin olive oil
- ¼ teaspoon salt
- Pinch black pepper
- 2 cloves garlic, minced
- 2 teaspoons lemon juice
- 2 teaspoons rosemary leaves, chopped
- Rosemary sprigs
- Capers

Directions:

1. In a bowl, combine oil, salt, pepper, garlic, lemon juice, and rosemary leaves. Brush onto the fish.
2. Grill over medium hot coals for 6 minutes. Top with rosemary sprigs and capers. Serve.

Dessert

Ricotta cheese in Lemon Zest

Ingredients:
- ½ cup ricotta cheese
- ¼ teaspoon vanilla extract
- ¼ teaspoon lemon zest, grated
- 1 package sugar substitute

Directions:
1. In a dessert bowl, combine ricotta cheese, vanilla extract, lemon zest, and sugar substitute. Serve chilled.

Day 3

Breakfast: Artichokes with Bacon and Egg

Midmorning snack: Mixed vegetables (carrots, green peas, and sweetcorn)

Lunch: Salmon in Cucumber Dill Dip

Midafternoon snack: Fat-free yogurt

Dinner: Skinless Chicken Saute

Dessert: Vanilla Ricotta Delight

Breakfast

Artichokes with Bacon and Egg

Ingredients:
- 2 medium artichokes
- 2 slices bacon
- 2 eggs

Directions:

1. In a deep saucepan, stand the artichokes. Cover and let it boil for 30 minutes. Turn artichokes to drain.

2. Spread the leaves open in a serving platter.

3. Meanwhile, cook the bacon in the skillet and poach the eggs in boiling salted water. Place the bacon slice into the artichoke with the poached eggs. Serve with vegetable juice cocktail.

Midmorning snack: Mixed vegetables (carrots, green peas, and corn)

Lunch

Salmon in Cucumber Dill Dip

Ingredients:
- 2 cups water
- ½ teaspoon granulated bouillon
- 1 celery, chopped
- 2 bay leaves
- 4 fresh dillweed

- 6 peppercorns
- 1 small lemon, sliced
- 6 salmon fillets

For the Cucumber-Dill Dip

Ingredients:
- 1/3 cup cucumber, finely chopped
- 1/3 cup plain yogurt fat-free
- 1/3 cup sour cream fat-free
- 1 teaspoon Dijon mustard
- 2 teaspoons fresh dill weed, chopped
- Dillweed sprigs

Directions:
1. In a skillet, combine the water, bouillon, celery, bay leaves, dillweed, peppercorns, and lemon. Bring to a boil and let it simmer for 10 minutes.
2. Add the salmon in the skillet and cook for 10 minutes.
3. Transfer to a platter and chill.
4. For the cucumber-dill dip: In a bowl, combine the cucumber, yogurt, sour cream, mustard, and fresh dill weed. Mix together until well combined.
5. Spoon the dip over the salmon and garnish with dillweed sprigs. Serve.

Midafternoon snack: Fat-free yogurt

Dinner

Skinless Chicken Saute

Ingredients:
- 2 tablespoons extra virgin olive oil
- 4 skinless chicken breast
- 1 onion, sliced
- 2 cloves garlic, minced
- 1 tablespoon rosemary leaves, chopped
- ½ cup fat-free chicken broth
- Pinch of salt
- Pinch of pepper

Directions:
1. In a skillet, heat the oil. Saute chicken breasts for 5 minutes.
2. Add the onions and cook for 3 minutes or until translucent.
3. Combine the garlic, rosemary leaves, chicken broth, salt, and pepper.
4. Cover and cook for 5 minutes whilst stirring occasionally. Serve.

Dessert

Vanilla Ricotta Delight

Ingredients:
- ½ cup ricotta cheese

- ¼ teaspoon vanilla extract
- 1 package sugar substitute

Directions:

In a dessert bowl, mix together the ricotta, vanilla extract, and sugar substitute. Serve chilled.

Day 4

Breakfast: Spinach Frittata
Midmorning snack: 1 celery stick with wedge non-fat cheese
Lunch: Chicken Salad in Fresh Lime
Mid afternoon snack: Fat-free yogurt
Dinner: Gingered Chicken
Dessert: 1 celery stick or mixed veggies

Breakfast

Spinach Frittata

Ingredients:
- 1 tablespoon extra-virgin olive oil
- 2 cloves garlic, minced
- 1 onion, sliced
- 1 package spinach
- 2 eggs
- 3 egg whites
- 1/3 cup fat-free evaporated milk

- ½ cup reduced-fat mozzarella cheese

Directions:

1. Preheat the oven to 350 F.
2. In a skillet, heat the oil and add the garlic and onion. Saute for 3 minutes or until tender.
3. Add the spinach and reduce to low.
4. Meanwhile, in a large bowl, beat the eggs and egg whites and milk. Mix until frothy.
5. Pour the egg mixture over the spinach. Cook for 5 minutes or until top is almost set. Sprinkle with cheese.

Midmorning snack: 1 celery stick with wedge non-fat cheese

Lunch

Chicken Salad in Fresh Lime

Ingredients:

For the salad:

- ½ cup pistachio nuts, finely ground
- ¼ teaspoon salt
- Pinch of salt
- 4 skinless chicken breast
- 2 tablespoons extra virgin olive oil
- ½ cup white onion, diced
- 1 romaine lettuce

For the dressing:

- 1 tablespoon white onion, grated
- 1 ripe avocado, peeled
- 3 tablespoons extra virgin olive oil
- 3 tablespoon fresh lime juice
- 1 tablespoon water

Directions:

1. For the salad, preheat the oven to 375 F.
2. In a bowl, mix the nuts, salt and pepper. Press the chicken into the nuts.
3. In a skillet, heat the oil and cook the coated chicken for 2 minutes. Place on a baking dish and bake for 15 minutes or until the juices run clear.
4. Heat the remaining oil and add the onion, salt, and pepper. Cook for 4 minutes or until the onions are browned.
5. For the dressing, in a blender, puree the onion, avocado, oil, lime juice, and water.
6. Place the lettuce on the plates and arrange the chicken. Serve with the dressing.

Mid afternoon snack: Fat-free yogurt

Dinner

Gingered Chicken

Ingredients:

- 1 tablespoon fresh lemon juice
- ½ teaspoon ground black pepper
- 1 ½ teaspoons fresh ginger, grated
- 2 cloves garlic
- 4 skinless chicken breast

Directions:

1. In a bowl, combine the lemon juice, pepper, ginger, and garlic. Mix well.
2. Pour the ginger mixture over the chicken and refrigerate for 1 hour.
3. In a skillet, heat the oil over a medium-high heat. Add the chicken and cook for 8 minutes or until golden brown. Serve.

Dessert: 1 celery stick or mixed veggies

Day 5

Breakfast: White Omelet

Midmorning snack: Hummus with raw vegetables

Lunch: South Beach Salad with Tuna

Midafternoon snack: Mixed raw nuts

Dinner: Roasted Vegetables

Dessert: 1 wedge non-fat cheese

Breakfast

White Omelet

Ingredients:
- 1 tablespoon scallions, chopped
- 1 tablespoon green bell pepper, chopped
- 1 tablespoon red bell peppers, chopped
- ½ cup liquid egg substitute
- 3 tablespoons reduced-fat cheese, shredded

Directions:
1. In a skillet, saute the scallions and peppers for 4 minutes or until tender.
2. Pour the egg substitute over the vegetables.
3. When partially set, spread the cheese on half of the egg and fold. Cook for 2 minutes or until cooked through. Serve.

Midmorning snack: Hummus with raw vegetables

Lunch

South Beach Salad with Tuna

Ingredients:

For the Salad:
- 1 can water-packed tuna
- 1/3 cup tomato, chopped
- 1/3 cup celery, chopped
- 1/3 cup cucumber, chopped

- 1/3 cup radishes, chopped
- 1 cup romaine lettuce, chopped

For the dressing:
- 4 teaspoons extra virgin olive oil
- 2 cloves garlic, finely chopped
- 2 tablespoons fresh lime juice
- 1/2 teaspoon black pepper

Directions:
1. In a bowl, layer the tuna, tomato, celery, cucumber, radishes, and lettuce.
2. For the dressing: Mix the olive oil, garlic, lime juice, and pepper. Drizzle over the salad and serve.

Midafternoon snack: Mixed raw nuts

Dinner

Roasted Vegetables

Ingredients:
- 1 summer squash, cut into bite-size pieces
- 1 yellow bell pepper, cut into bite-size pieces
- 1 red bell pepper, cut into bite-size pieces
- 1 zucchini, cut into bite-size pieces
- 1 lb asparagus, cut into bite-size pieces

- 1 red onion
- 1 teaspoon salt
- 3 tablespoons extra virgin olive oil
- ½ teaspoon pepper

Directions:

1. Heat the oven to 450 F.
2. In a roasting pan, place the squash, peppers, zucchini, asparagus, and onion. Toss with oil, salt, and pepper. Mix well.
3. Spread in the pan and roast for 30 minutes or until vegetables are tender.

Dessert: 1 wedge non-fat cheese

Day 6

Breakfast: Salmon Frittata

Midmorning snack: Hummus with raw vegetables

Lunch: Yummy Flank Steak

Midafternoon snack: Wedge of low-fat cheese

Dinner: Grilled Steak with Tomato

Dessert: 1 celery or carrot stick

Breakfast

Salmon Frittata

Ingredients:

- 1 tablespoon extra-virgin olive oil
- 8 stalks asparagus
- ½ onion
- ¼ cup sun dried tomatoes
- 2 oz smoked salmon
- ½ cup liquid egg substitute
- ¼ cup water
- 3 tablespoons non-fat dry milk
- ¼ teaspoon fresh marjoram
- Pinch of pepper
- Fat-free sour cream

Directions:

1. In a large skillet, boil water. Add the asparagus and cook until tender.
2. Coat the oven with cooking spray and add the olive oil. Saute until tender and translucent.
3. Add the asparagus and sun-dried tomatoes. Add the smoked salmon and remove from heat.
4. Combine the egg substitute, water, dry milk, marjoram, and pepper. Pour over the salmon mixture. Cover and cook on low for 7 minutes or until set.
5. Place the skillet under the broiler until the frittata is puffed up.
6. Top the frittata with sour cream. Serve.

Midmorning snack: Hummus with raw vegetables

Lunch

Yummy Flank Steak

Ingredients:
- 1 ½ lbs flank steak
- ¼ cup Worcestershire sauce
- 1 tablespoon lemon juice
- ½ cup tomato juice
- 1 onion, finely chopped
- 1 clove garlic, minced
- 1/8 teaspoon salt
- ½ teaspoon pepper

Directions:
1. Place the steak in a baking dish. Combine the Worcestershire sauce, lemon juice, tomato juice, onion, garlic, salt, and pepper. Pour the mixture over the steak and refrigerate for 1 hour.
2. Place the steak on the broiler and add some marinade. Broil 3 inches from the heat for 5 minutes. Turn and then brush again with the marinade. Broil for 3 minutes. Serve.

Midafternoon snack: Wedge of low-fat cheese

Dinner

Grilled Steak with Tomato

Ingredients:
- 6 oz sirloin steaks
- 2 tomatoes, halved
- 2 tablespoons extra virgin olive oil
- 1 garlic clove, minced
- 1 onion, chopped
- ¼ cup fresh basil
- Pinch of salt
- Pinch of pepper

Directions:
1. On a greased grill over medium hot coals, place the steak. Cook until browned on the outside for 15 minutes.
2. Place the tomatoes on the grill and brush with oil. Grill until browned for 3 minutes.
3. In a pan, put the oil, garlic, and onion. Cook for 5 minutes or until tender. Add the basil.
4. When tomatoes are soft, add the onion mixture then set aside to cool.
5. When the steak is done, put on a platter. Spoon the tomato relish. Season with salt and pepper. Cut into thin slices and serve.

Dessert: 1 celery or carrot stick

Day 7

Breakfast: Spinach and Tomato Frittata

Midmorning snack: 1 cup fat-free yogurt

Lunch: Spinach Salad

Midafternoon snack: Raw nuts (almond, walnuts)

Dinner: Butternut Squash Soup

Dessert: 1 wedge low-fat cheese, a glass non-fat milk

Breakfast

Spinach and Tomato Frittata

Ingredients:

For the frittata
- 1 tablespoon olive oil
- 1 small onion, sliced
- 1 clove garlic, minced
- 1 package spinach
- 1 cup applesauce
- 1/3 cup coconut milk
- ½ cup Tofutti cheese

For the Salsa
- 4 tomatoes, chopped
- 2 green onions, minced
- 2 tablespoons fresh cilantro minced
- 1 clove garlic, minced
- 1 tablespoon lime juice

- 1/8 teaspoon pepper
- ¼ teaspoon salt

Directions:

1. For the frittata: Preheat the oven to 350 F.
2. Heat the oil in a skillet. Add the onion and garlic and cook. Stir for 3 minutes. Add the spinach.
3. Meanwhile, pour the applesauce and milk in a large bowl. Whisk until foamy.
4. Pour the applesauce mixture over the spinach and cook for 8 minutes. Drizzle some cheese.
5. Bake for 10 minutes or until cheese has melted.
6. For the salsa, combine tomatoes, onions, cilantro, garlic, lime juice, pepper, and salt in a large bowl. Serve and pour over the frittata.

Midmorning snack: 1 cup fat-free yogurt

Lunch

Spinach Salad

Ingredients:

- 2 teaspoons vegetable oil
- 1 ½ teaspoons sugar
- Dash of Worcestershire sauce
- 4 teaspoons balsamic vinegar
- 3 cups loosely packed spinach

- ½ cup tomatoes
- 1 oz Tofutti cheese

Midafternoon snack: Raw nuts (almond, walnuts)

Dinner

Butternut Squash Soup

Ingredients:
- 1 butternut squash, cut into halves
- 1 onion, sliced
- Vegetable broth
- ¼ teaspoon dried marjoram
- ¼ teaspoon dried rosemary
- 2 cups water
- Pinch of Salt
- Pinch of pepper
- 1 tablespoon parsley, chopped

Directions:
1. Combine squash, onion, vegetable broth, rosemary, water, salt and pepper in a large saucepan. Bring to a boil. Let it simmer for 45 minutes uncovered.
2. In a blender, puree the soup and transfer to the saucepan.
3. Bring to a boil and let simmer for 3 minutes.
4. Serve with grilled fish or mixed veggies.

Dessert: 1 wedge low-fat cheese, a glass non-fat milk

Chapter 6 – Meal Plans for Phase Two of the South Beach Diet

Phase Two is considered to be the most liberal of the three Phases. This is the stage where you start reintroducing certain carbs into the diet again, especially fruits, whole grain bread, whole grain pasta, rice, and potatoes. Many dieters of the South Beach Diet stay longer on Phase One than the official 2 week period because they believe they lose more weight than Phase Two would permit, and believe that moving to Phase Two would slow down their progress towards their target weight loss goal. Remaining on Phase One for much longer than the two weeks is allowed but not encouraged.

Phase One is not advised for a long term diet. When you reach your target goal during Phase One and are able to resolve your insulin resistance, you should move on to a lon- term weight loss program, which is Phase Two. There will be days when you will slip or overindulge. When this happens, you are free to go back to Phase One so you can lose the pounds that you have gained. This is how flexible the South Beach Diet is.

The following is an example of Phase Two's meal plan:

Day 1

Breakfast: Oatmeal Pancake

Lunch: Roasted Cauliflower Florets

Dinner: Zucchini Spaghetti

Breakfast

Oatmeal Pancake

Ingredients:

- ½ cup oatmeal
- ¼ cup low fat cottage cheese
- ¼ teaspoon cinnamon
- 1 teaspoon vanilla extract
- 4 egg whites
- ¼ teaspoon nutmeg

Directions:

1. In a blender, process the oatmeal, cheese, vanilla extract, egg whites, and nutmeg. Blend until smooth.
2. In a skillet, add the batter and cook until both sides are browned.
3. Top the pancakes with maple syrup or low-fat syrup. Pair with 1 glass of orange juice.

Lunch

Roasted Cauliflower Florets

Ingredients:

- 3 cups cauliflower florets
- 4 tablespoons olive oil
- ¼ cup breadcrumbs

Directions:

1. Preheat the oven to 400 F.
2. Put the cauliflower and drip with oil in a baking dish. Drizzle with olive oil and breadcrumbs. Spread evenly in a

single layer.

3. Bake for 25 minutes. Serve hot.

Dinner

Zucchini Spaghetti

Ingredients:
- Spaghetti squash, seeded and halved lengthwise
- 2 ½ tablespoons olive oil
- 2 red onion, sliced
- 1 zucchini
- 4 tomatoes, cubed
- ¼ teaspoon salt
- ¼ teaspoon pepper
- 1 lemon, sliced

Directions:
1. Place the halved squash in a baking dish. Add ¼ cup of water. Wrap with plastic wrap. Put the dish on the microwave and set for 10 minutes on high or until tender. Remove and let cool.
2. Meanwhile, in a skillet, warm the oil and cook the onion. Sauté for 3 minutes. Toss the zucchini and cook for 5 minutes or until browned.
3. Toss the tomatoes, salt, and pepper. Let simmer for 10 minutes.

4. Transfer the squash strands in a platter. Put the remaining oil. Pile the squash in the center and put a spoonful of veggie mix around the squash. Add the slices of lemon.

Day 2

Breakfast: Veggie Panini Cheese Melt

Lunch: Grilled Tofutti Flatbreads with Veggies

Dinner: Broccoli with Pumpkin Seeds

Breakfast

Veggie Panini Cheese Melt

Ingredients:
- 2 slices whole wheat bread
- 1 teaspoon deli mustard
- 1 ½ ounces low-fat cheese
- 7 red and yellow bell peppers, grilled
- 7 asparagus spears, grilled

Directions:

1. Spread the mustard over each slice of whole wheat bread. Put cheese on top. Place the asparagus and bell peppers on top of the cheese, and then the second bread and mustard.
2. Heat the panini press and spray with oil. Put the sandwich on the plate and close.

3. Grill the sandwich for 5 minutes or until the cheese is melted. Serve hot.

Lunch

Grilled Tofutti Flatbreads with Veggies

Ingredients:
- 1 tablespoon olive oil
- Pinch of salt
- ½ teaspoon dried oregano
- 8 oz mushrooms, sliced
- 1 small zucchini, halved lengthwise
- 1 cup grape tomatoes
- 1 onion, thinly sliced
- 3 Roti bread
- ½ cup Tofutti cheese

Directions:
1. Combine ½ teaspoon oil, salt, and oregano in a bowl.
2. Meanwhile, mix mushrooms, zucchini, tomatoes, ½ teaspoon oil, and salt in another bowl.
3. Grill vegetables over medium heat for 10 minutes or until tender. Shake and turn occasionally to keep vegetables from burning, and then remove.
4. Coat the sides of the dough with oil and put on the grill. Grill until lightly browned. Top the bread with grilled vegetables and Tofutti cheese. Grill for another 3 minutes. Serve.

Dinner

Broccoli with Pumpkin Seeds

Ingredients:
- 4 cups broccoli florets
- 1 teaspoon olive oil
- 1 tablespoon maple syrup
- 1 tablespoon vinegar
- Pinch of pepper
- Pinch of salt
- ¼ cup pumpkin seeds

Directions:
1. Put 1/3 cup of water in a skillet and let it boil. Add the broccoli. Cover and cook for 3 minutes. Then, cook, uncovered, for another 3 minutes or until the water begins to evaporate.
2. Add olive oil and combine the broccoli. Cook for 2 minutes and then remove.
3. Drizzle with maple syrup and vinegar. Add red pepper and salt. Toss to coat. Top with pumpkin seeds.

Day 3

Breakfast: Veggie Quiche

Lunch: Spinach-Filled Mushrooms

Dinner: Chicken Braised in Wine Sauce

Breakfast

Veggie Quiche

Ingredients:
- 10 oz spinach, thawed
- ¼ cup red bell peppers
- ¾ cup liquid egg substitute
- ¾ cup reduced-fat cheese, shredded
- ¼ cup onions, chopped

Directions:
1. Put the spinach into the microwave for 2 minutes. Drain excess liquid.
2. Line a muffin pan and spray with cooking spray.
3. In a large bowl, combine red bell peppers, egg substitute, cheese, onions, and spinach. Mix well.

Lunch

Spinach-Filled Mushrooms

Ingredients:
- 8 large mushrooms
- ½ cup water
- 1/8 teaspoon salt
- 1 package spinach
- 1 tablespoon extra-virgin olive oil

Directions:

1. Wash the mushrooms and trim the ends.
2. Add 1/2 cup of water in a medium saucepan and bring to a boil. Add salt and spinach. Put the spinach in a blender and process until smooth.
3. In a large skillet, heat the oil. Add the mushrooms and saute until golden brown. Remove.
4. Put the mushroom caps and sauté for 4 minutes. Place in a platter.
5. Drain and combine sautéed mushrooms. Spoon spinach mixture over the mushrooms. Serve.

Dinner

Chicken Braised in Wine Sauce

Ingredients:
- 4 tablespoons extra virgin olive oil
- 1 clove garlic, minced
- 4 boneless chicken breast, cut into strips
- ¼ teaspoon salt
- ¼ teaspoon pepper
- ¼ cup dry white wine
- 2 tomatoes, sliced

Directions:

1. Heat the oil in a skillet. Add the garlic and cook for 3 minutes. Put the chicken and add salt and pepper. Cook

for 10 minutes.
2. Add the white wine and cook for another 3 minutes.
3. Remove chicken and put in a platter.
4. In the same skillet, saute the tomatoes for 3 minutes. Place over the chicken. Drizzle with chicken drippings.

Day 4

Breakfast: Quinoa and Edamame Salad
Lunch: Chicken Packets with Veggies
Dinner: Veggie Greens Soup

Breakfast

Quinoa and Edamame Salad

Ingredients:
- 2 cups quinoa, cooked
- 2 cups edamame, cooked
- 2 tablespoons coconut, shredded
- ½ cup sliced almonds
- 1 tablespoon extra-virgin olive oil
- ¼ cup balsamic vinegar
- ½ teaspoon salt
- ½ cup almonds, toasted

Directions:

1. Combine the quinoa, edamame, coconut, and almonds in a bowl.
2. For the dressing: Whisk together oil, vinegar, and salt. Pour over the mixture.
3. Cover and chill for 1 hour. Serve

Lunch

Chicken Packets with Veggies

Ingredients:
- 1/3 cup dry sherry
- 2 teaspoons sesame oil
- 1 teaspoon garlic, finely chopped
- ¼ cup green onions, finely chopped
- 1 teaspoon ginger, grated
- 4 boneless chicken breasts, cut into strips
- 1 red bell pepper, sliced
- 1 o oz snow peas
- 10 oz broccoli florets
- 1 red bell pepper, sliced
- 5 oz chestnuts

Directions:
1. Preheat the oven to 450 F.
2. In a bowl, mix the sherry, oil, garlic, onions, and ginger.

3. Add the chicken breast, bell pepper, snow peas, broccoli, bell pepper, and chestnuts. Toss until well coated.

4. Center chicken on each four sheets of aluminum foil, double fold the sides, and seal with packets. Bake for 15 minutes. Serve.

Dinner

Veggie Greens Soup

Ingredients:
- 2 tablespoons extra virgin olive oil
- 5 leeks, thinly sliced
- 4 cloves garlic, sliced
- 1 teaspoon dried tarragon
- ½ teaspoon salt
- ½ teaspoon pepper
- 5 cups vegetable stock
- 4 cups Swiss chard leaves

Directions:
1. Heat the oil in a skillet over medium heat. Toss the leeks for 5 minutes. Add the garlic, tarragon, salt, and pepper. Saute for 1 minute.

2. Pour 2 cups of stock and bring to a boil.

3. Stir the remaining 4 cups. Add the Swiss chard in batches. Cook on high for 15 minutes.

4. Using a food processor, pulp. Spoon into individual serving bowls.

Day 5

Breakfast: Strawberries and Arugula Salad
Lunch: Brussels Sprouts Delight
Dinner: Pan-Fried Veggies

Breakfast

Strawberries and Arugula Salad

Ingredients:

Strawberries Preserve

- 1 ½ tablespoons water
- 5 oz strawberries, sliced
- 1 tablespoon balsamic vinegar
- ½ tablespoon pepper

For the Vinaigrette

- 1 ¼ tablespoons lemon juice
- 1 ½ tablespoons white wine vinegar
- ½ cup extra-virgin olive oil
- 1 ¼ tablespoons black pepper

For the Salad

- 4 oz arugula leaves
- 4 oz watercress leaves

- strawberries, halved
- pinch black pepper

Directions:

1. For the strawberry preserves: Mix water, strawberries, vinegar, and pepper. Cook for 25 minutes in a saucepan or until the mixture is a little thick. Set aside and refrigerate.
2. For the vinaigrette: Combine lemon juice and vinegar in a bowl. Whisk oil and pepper. Stir well. Set aside.
3. Combine arugula and watercress in a salad bowl. Pour over the vinaigrette. Dip the sides of strawberry halves in pepper. Place them around the greens. Serve.

Lunch

Brussels Sprouts Delight

Ingredients:

- 1 lb brussels sprouts
- 1 teaspoon olive oil
- ½ yellow onion, finely chopped
- ½ teaspoon ground black pepper

Directions:

1. Preheat the oven to 425 F. Place a steamer basket in a pot and line a baking sheet. Add water. Bring to a boil.
2. Place the brussels sprouts in the steamer. Steam for 4 minutes or until barely tender.

3. Remove from pot. Drain. Transfer to a large bowl and drizzle olive oil, onion, and pepper. Coat well.
4. Spread the vegetables and bake for 20 minutes. Serve.

Dinner

Pan-Fried Veggies

Ingredients:
- 3 tablespoons vegetable oil
- 1 package green beans
- 1 package broccoli
- 1 package red bell peppers
- 1 package mushrooms
- 2 tablespoons water
- 2 tablespoons soy sauce
- 1 package fresh spinach

Directions:
1. Heat 1 ½ tablespoons olive oil in a large skillet. Add green peas, broccoli, bell peppers, and mushrooms. Stir fry for about 7 minutes. Add water and soy sauce. Stir-fry for another 5 minutes. Toss the spinach.
2. Cover and let steam for 3 minutes over medium heat. Turn the spinach once. Steam for another 3 minutes.
3. Pour the vegetables in platter. Serve.

Day 6

Breakfast: Spinach Loaf
Lunch: Black Rice Salad
Dinner: Braised Veggies in Balsamic Vinegar

Breakfast

Spinach Loaf

Ingredients:
- 1 ½ teaspoon baking powder
- 250g almond flour
- ¼ teaspoon baking soda
- ¼ teaspoon salt
- 2 bunches spinach
- 1 cup applesauce
- 1 teaspoon lemon juice
- 60ml coconut milk
- 1 tablespoon apple cider vinegar
- 1 tablespoon olive oil

Directions:
1. Preheat the oven to 345 F.
2. Line a loaf tin with baking paper.
3. Combine baking powder, almond flour, baking soda, and salt in a bowl. Put the spinach leaves in a food processor. Mix together the applesauce, lemon juice, coconut milk, apple cider vinegar, and oil. Mix thoroughly.

4. Spoon mixture into the loaf tin. Bake for 45 minutes. Remove and let cool.

Lunch

Black Rice Salad

Ingredients:

For the dressing:
- ½ cup apple cider vinegar
- 1 tablespoon garlic, minced
- 1 tablespoon ground cumin
- Pinch of salt
- Pinch of pepper
- ¼ cup and 2 tablespoons olive oil

For the salad:
- 4 cups gluten-free stock
- 2 cups black rice
- 1 tablespoon olive oil
- 1 cup grape tomatoes
- Pinch of salt
- Pinch of pepper
- 1 cup edamame beans, sliced
- ½ cup onion, sliced
- 1/3 cup cilantro, chopped
- 2 cups burrata cheese

Directions:

1. For the dressing: Place the vinegar, garlic, cumin, salt, and pepper in a blender. Add the oil and blend on high. Set aside and store in the refrigerator.
2. Meanwhile, preheat the oven to 375 F.
3. For the salad: Pour the gluten-free stock in a large saucepan. Bring to a boil. Add the black rice. Cook for 50 minutes. Transfer to a bowl. Set aside.
4. Put a tablespoon of oil on a baking tray. Place grape tomatoes on it. Add salt and pepper to taste. Roast tomatoes for 25 minutes.
5. Add edamame beans, onions, cilantro, and tomatoes to the rice. Mix well. Add burrata cheese to the salad. Pour the dressing onto the salad. Toss until well coated. Serve.

Dinner

Braised Veggies in Balsamic Vinegar

Ingredients:

- 1 tablespoon olive oil
- 1 clove garlic, chopped
- 1 small onion, chopped
- ¼ cup celery, thinly sliced
- ½ cup green bell pepper, chopped
- 3 cups tomatoes, chopped
- 1 tablespoon balsamic vinegar
- 1/8 teaspoon ground black pepper

Directions:

1. Heat the oil in a nonstick skillet. Sauté the garlic, onion, celery, and bell pepper for 5 minutes.
2. Add tomatoes, vinegar, and pepper. Bring to a boil. Let simmer for 10 minutes. Serve.

Day 7

Breakfast: Egg Pancetta

Lunch: Chicken Chipotle

Dinner: Baked Tomatoes with Tofutti Cheese

Breakfast

Egg Pancetta

Ingredients:

- 3 large eggs
- 3 tablespoons onions, chopped
- 3 pieces pancetta, crumbled
- ¼ cup cheese blend, shredded

Directions:

1. Heat the oven to 450 F.
2. Line a baking sheet with baking parchment. Set aside.
3. In a bowl, add the egg whites. Mix well. Add onions, pancetta, and cheese.
4. Put the egg mixture onto the parchment. Make a well in the middle. Bake for 3 minutes. Remove. Drop yolks into

the well.

5. Return the pan to the oven and bake for 4 minutes. Remove and serve immediately.

Lunch

Chicken Chipotle

Ingredients:
- 3 tablespoons olive oil
- 1 onion, chopped
- 1 pasilla pepper, diced
- Pinch of salt
- Pinch of pepper
- 3 chipotles chiles en adobo, chopped
- 3 garlic cloves, chopped
- 2 tomatoes, diced
- 1 teaspoon ground cumin
- 6 cups of water
- 1 whole chicken
- 1 lime
- 20 corn tortillas
- Low-fat sour cream

Directions:

1. Heat the olive oil in a large stock pot. Put onion and pasillas. Cook for 7 minutes. Put salt and pepper to taste.

Add chipotles and garlic. Cook for 3 minutes.

2. Add tomatoes, cumin, water, and chicken. Bring to a boil for 30 minutes. Remove chicken from pot and let cool. Save the solids and pour the liquid in a bowl. Cool the broth.
3. Remove skin and bones of the chicken. Put the reserved vegetables. Squeeze in lime over the mixture.
4. Meanwhile, warm the tortilla in a nonstick pan. Spoon a tablespoon of chicken mixture and grill the tortilla. Secure it with a toothpick at the seam.
5. Deep fry until brown and crisp. Remove the toothpicks. Serve with sour cream.

Dinner

Baked Tomatoes with Tofutti Cheese

Ingredients:
- 3 large tomatoes, halved
- ¼ cup marjoram
- ¼ cup basil
- ¼ cup parsley
- ½ cup grated bread crumbs
- ½ cup Tofutti cheese
- 2 cloves garlic, minced
- 3 tablespoons extra virgin olive oil
- Pinch of salt
- Pinch of pepper

Directions:

1. Preheat the oven to 350 F. Put tomatoes in a baking dish.
2. Combine marjoram, basil, parsley, bread crumbs, cheese, garlic, oil, salt, and pepper in a bowl. Mix well.
3. Put each tomato with a good portion of the mixture. Bake for 40 minutes. Serve.

Chapter 7 – Meal Plans for Phase Three of the South Beach Diet

You have come this far and have probably reached your ideal weight. If you have been religiously following Phases One to Two, you must have an improved blood chemistry by now. Phase Three is meant to help you maintain your weight and will show how you will eat for the rest of your life. The Third Phase will be your diet for life.

This is considered the most liberal stage in that you will not view this Phase as a diet plan, but a lifestyle. You will no longer see this phase as a weight loss regimen but something that is part of your everyday life. It is at this point that you have become more accustomed to the South Beach Diet and already know how it works and how it affects the body. If you backslide a little, go back to Phases One and Two. Remember, this diet is designed with flexibility in mind.

The following recipes that you will see in this Phase now include multigrain and rice. At this point, you know well which carbs to avoid and which ones are good for the body. Just as with Phase Two, you will be forgoing the two daytime snacks, but still get to enjoy chocolate cakes. Just remember to eat in moderation.

Day 1

Breakfast: Veggie Toast

Lunch: Chicken Salad Topped with Feta Cheese

Dinner: Braised Apples and Cabbage

Dessert: Onion Marmalade and Blue Cheese Ice Cream

Breakfast

Veggie Toast

Ingredients:
- 2 leeks, chopped
- 3 zucchini, sliced
- 2 green peppers, sliced
- 2 tablespoons extra virgin olive oil
- Pesto
- 50g pistachios
- 25g Parmesan cheese, grated
- 1 thick slice wheat bread
- 1 tablespoon olive oil

Directions:
1. Preheat the oven to 400 F.
2. Combine leeks, zucchini, pepper, oil, and pesto in a bowl. Spread over ovenproof dish. Bake for 25 minutes. Stir and bake for another 15 minutes.
3. Combine pistachios, cheese, bread, and oil in a food processor until it forms a rough crumb. Top veggies with crumbs. Bake for 15 minutes or until golden brown.

Lunch

Chicken Salad Topped with Feta Cheese

For the dressing:

Ingredients:
- ½ cup balsamic vinegar

- 2 tablespoons honey
- 1 teaspoon dried ginger
- ½ teaspoon ground cumin
- 2 tablespoon olive oil
- Black pepper to taste

For the salad:
- 1 tablespoon olive oil
- 1 large chicken breast, unseasoned
- Pinch of Salt
- Pinch of pepper
- 3 oz green salad mix
- ½ cup almonds
- 2 cups strawberries
- 4 oz feta cheese

Directions:

1. For the dressing: Add vinegar, honey, ginger, and cumin on a food processor. Drizzle olive oil while processing. Add the pepper.
2. For the salad: Heat the grill. Rub chicken with olive oil on both sides. Add salt and pepper to taste.
3. Once grilled, cut chicken into strips.
4. Meanwhile, add salad greens, almonds, strawberries, and feta cheese in a salad bowl. Pour balsamic dressing. Toss gently. Serve.

Dinner

Braised Apples and Cabbage

Ingredients:
- 2 tablespoons extra virgin olive oil
- 2 onions, thinly sliced
- 2 apples, chopped
- 4 cloves garlic, chopped
- 1 piece cinnamon stick
- ½ teaspoon black peppercorns
- ½ teaspoon sea salt
- 1 small red cabbage, shredded
- 2 tablespoons water
- 3 tablespoons balsamic vinegar
- 2 tablespoons coconut sugar

Directions:
1. Heat the oil in a skillet. Add the onions and cook for 4 minutes.
2. Add the apples, garlic, cinnamon stick, peppercorns, and salt. Stir for 2 minutes and add the cabbage in batches.
3. Pour in water, vinegar, and sugar.
4. Transfer everything into the saucepan. Cook for 45 minutes. Discard cinnamon stick.

Dessert

Onion Marmalade and Blue Cheese Ice Cream

Ingredients:
- 300ml almond milk
- 300 ml coconut whipping cream
- 3 peppercorns
- 2 cloves garlic
- 1 cup applesauce
- 125g vegetarian blue cheese

For the marmalade:
- 2 red onions, thinly sliced
- 2 tablespoons sugar
- 1 tablespoon sherry vinegar

Directions:
1. In a saucepan, warm almond milk, cream, peppercorns, and garlic. Let cool for 15 minutes. Combine the appleasauce. Mix well.
2. Return to the pan and stir until the mixture thickens. Add cheese in batches. Let cool.
3. Pour mixture into a container and freeze. Once partly frozen, mix and return to the freezer. Repeat the procedure 3 times.
4. For the red onion marmalade: Saute onions for 2 minutes. Add sugar and vinegar. Let it boil for 7 minutes. Store in a jar. This is best served either hot or cold.

Day 2

Breakfast: Frittaflle
Lunch: Carrot and Radish Salad
Dinner: Butternut Squash Soup
Dessert: Cinnamon Bread

Breakfast

Frittaflle

Ingredients:
- 1 tablespoon olive oil
- 1 red bell pepper, diced
- 2 cups potatoes, roasted and cubed
- 2 cups arugula
- 4 pieces bacon, broken into pieces
- 4 large eggs
- ½ cup parmesan
- Pinch of salt
- Pinch of pepper
- 1 cup mozzarella cheese

Directions:
1. Preheat the oven to 375 F. Add olive oil in a skillet. Add red peppers and saute for 2 minutes. Toss the potatoes for 2 minutes. Add arugula and bacon. Saute for 4 minutes.

2. Meanwhile, in a bowl, combine eggs, cheese, salt, and pepper. Mix well. Pour the mixture over the pan and put in ¾ cup mozzarella cheese. Cook for 3 minutes.
3. Transfer to the oven and bake for 10 minutes at 375 F. Remove and put on a wire rack. Let cool for 45 minutes.
4. Meanwhile, heat a waffle iron. Place the frittata on it and heat until warm. Serve.

Lunch

Carrot and Radish Salad

Ingredients:
- ½ package penne pasta
- Handful string beans
- 2 carrots, diced
- 5 radishes, sliced
- 1 stalk celery
- Dash of mustard powder
- ½ juice from lemon
- 2 tablespoons extra virgin olive oil
- 1 teaspoon sea salt
- 1 teaspoon ground pepper

Directions:
1. Cook the pasta according to manufacturer's directions.
2. Add string beans before the pasta cooks.
3. Strain both pasta and beans. Put in a large salad bowl.

4. Combine carrot, radish, celery, mustard powder, lemon, oil, salt and pepper. Serve.

Dinner

Butternut Squash Soup

Ingredients:
- 1 butternut squash, halved
- 1 onion, chopped
- ¼ teaspoon dried marjoram
- ¼ teaspoon dried rosemary
- 2 cups water
- Vegetable broth
- 2 slices whole wheat bread, crumbled
- Pinch of salt
- Pinch of pepper
- 1 tablespoon parsley, chopped

Directions:
1. Put together squash, onion, marjoram, rosemary, water, broth, bread, salt and pepper in a saucepan. Bring to a boil. Let it simmer for 30 minutes uncovered.
2. In a blender, puree the soup. Put into the saucepan. Bring to a boil and let simmer for 3 minutes.
3. Sprinkle with parsley. Serve.

Dessert

Cinnamon Bread

Ingredients:
- Unsalted butter
- 4 teaspoons ground cinnamon
- 3 tablespoons sugar
- ¾ teaspoon xanthan gum
- 1 teaspoon baking soda
- 2 cups all-purpose flour
- ¼ teaspoon salt
- 1 cup sugar
- ½ cup unsalted butter
- 2 eggs
- 1 teaspoon pure vanilla extract
- 1 cup buttermilk
- ½ cup chopped pecans

Directions:
1. Preheat the oven to 350 F.
2. Grease a loaf pan with unsalted butter.
3. For the filling, combine cinnamon and sugar. Mix until well combined. Set aside.
4. For the bread, combine xanthan gum, baking soda, flour, and salt. Mix. Set aside.
5. Mix together sugar and butter and put in an electric mixer. Stir until fluffy. Add eggs and vanilla.

6. Combine the buttermilk and flour mixture to the sugar mixture. Mix well and then fold in the pecans.
7. Spoon a third of the batter into the loaf pan. Sprinkle cinnamon sugar to serve as filling. Bake for 45 minutes or until golden brown.

Day 3

Breakfast: Mozzarella and Swiss Chard Omelet
Lunch: Berries Combo in Cilantro Vinaigrette
Dinner: Broccoli and Mushroom Pizza
Dessert: Granola Oatmeal Cookie

Breakfast

Mozzarella and Swiss Chard Omelet

Ingredients:
- 1 teaspoon olive oil
- ½ tablespoon garlic, minced
- ½ cup Swiss chard leaves, julienned
- 2 tablespoons mozzarella cheese

Directions:
1. Heat the oil in a skillet. Add the garlic and cook for 3 minutes or until fragrant.
2. Toss Swiss chard. Cook for 2 minutes. Set aside.
3. Make an omelet with chard leaves and mozzarella as filling.

Lunch

Berries Combo in Cilantro Vinaigrette

Ingredients:

For the dressing:
- 1 ½ cup cilantro leaves
- ¼ cup rice wine vinegar
- ¼ cup pure mirin
- 1 tablespoon ginger, grated
- Pinch of salt

For the salad:
- 1 package baby spinach
- ¼ cup strawberries
- ¼ cup blueberries
- ¼ cup fresh raspberries
- Lime wedges

Directions:

1. For the dressing: Mix cilantro, vinegar, mirin, ginger, and salt in a blender. Process until mixed well.
2. For the salad: Put the spinach in a salad bowl. Toss strawberries, blueberries, and raspberries.
3. Pour the pureed mixture onto the salad. Serve with lime wedges.

Dinner

Broccoli and Mushroom Pizza

Ingredients:
- 1 tablespoon olive oil
- 2 cups broccoli florets
- 2 cups mushrooms, sliced
- 1 onion, chopped
- 1 red bell pepper, cut into strips
- 12-ounce package pizza dough
- 1 cup tomato sauce
- ½ cup mozzarella cheese

Directions:
1. Preheat the oven to 450 F. Grease baking sheet with olive oil.
2. Meanwhile, in a skillet, heat the oil. Cook the broccoli, mushrooms, onion, and bell pepper. Stir for 3 minutes or until tender. Set aside.
3. Put the pizza dough on the baking sheet. Spread tomato sauce and top with cooked veggies. Sprinkle cheese.
4. Bake for 25 minutes or until the crust is baked through. Serve.

Dessert

Granola Oatmeal Cookie

Ingredients:
- 3 cups rolled oats

- 1 teaspoon cinnamon
- ½ cup coconut sugar
- ¼ cup almond butter
- ½ teaspoon salt
- 2 teaspoons pure vanilla extract
- 1/3 cup maple syrup
- ½ cup gluten-free chocolate chips

Directions:

1. Preheat the oven to 325 F.
2. In a large bowl, combine, cinnamon, sugar, butter, and salt. Stir in vanilla extract and maple syrup.
3. Pour onto the baking sheet. Bake for 45 minutes. Stir every 5 minutes so the granola won't burn.
4. Once the granola is turned golden brown, put chocolate chips on top. Let cool and serve.

Day 4

Breakfast: Herbed Omelet
Lunch: Cucumber Noodle Salad
Dinner: Lemon Fish
Dessert: Strawberry Cream Donut

Breakfast

Herbed Omelet

Ingredients:

- 1 teaspoon extra virgin olive oil
- 3 large eggs
- 1 tablespoon thyme, finely chopped
- 1 tablespoon basil, finely chopped
- 1 tablespoon parsley, finely chopped
- 1 tablespoon rosemary, finely chopped
- Pinch of salt
- Pinch of pepper

Directions:

1. Heat oil in a pan over low heat.
2. Whisk eggs, thyme, basil, parsley, rosemary, salt, and pepper in a bowl until a bit frothy.
3. Pour the mixture into the pan. Cook for 1 minute and flip to cook the other side. Fold the empty half over. Cook for 2 minutes. Transfer to a plate and serve.

Lunch

Cucumber Noodle Salad

Ingredients:

For the dressing:

- 1 teaspoon cup olive oil
- 1/3 cup vanilla almond milk, unsweetened
- ¼ teaspoon garlic powder
- 2 teaspoons lemon juice

- ½ teaspoon lemon zest
- ¼ teaspoon salt
- 1 teaspoon poppy seeds
- 1 tablespoon maple syrup

For the salad:
- 1 apple
- ½ avocado
- 1/3 cup cashews, roasted
- ½ cucumber, julienned
- 2 cups spinach

Directions:

1. For the dressing: Combine oil, milk, garlic powder, lemon juice and zest, salt, poppy seeds, and maple syrup. Put in a food processor. Blend for 2 minutes.

2. For the salad: Pour the dressing in the salad bowl. Toss the apple, avocado, cashews, and cucumber. Top with spinach. Toss well and serve.

Dinner

Lemon Fish

Ingredients:
- 5 large fillet fish
- ¼ cup onion, chopped
- ¼ cup carrots, diced

- ¼ cup celery, diced
- 2 tablespoons parsley, chopped
- 2 lemons, thinly sliced

Directions:

1. Heat the oven to 350 F. Place 1 fish fillet in the middle of the foil. Top with onions, carrots, celery, and parsley. Pour over lemon slices.
2. Fold the foil and place on a baking sheet. Bake for 20 minutes. Serve.

Dessert

Strawberry Cream Donut

Ingredients:

For the donuts:
- Coconut oil
- 1 cup strawberries, chopped
- 1 tablespoon sugar
- ½ teaspoon xanthan gum
- ½ cup teff flour
- ¾ teaspoon baking powder
- 1 cup almond flour, blanched
- ¼ teaspoon baking soda
- Pinch of salt
- ¼ cup coconut milk

- ½ tablespoons vanilla bean paste
- 5 tablespoons butter, unsalted
- 1 egg

Directions:

1. Preheat the oven to 350 F. Grease a donut pan with oil. Set aside.
2. Combine strawberries and sugar in a food processor. Blend until smooth. Set aside.
3. Meanwhile, combine xanthan gum, teff flour, baking powder, almond flour, baking soda, and salt in a bowl.
4. Put together coconut milk, vanilla bean paste, and the strawberry puree in a different bowl.
5. In a mixer, beat butter and sugar for 2 minutes. Add the egg.
6. Gradually add coconut milk and flour blend. Beat until well blended.
7. Scoop batter into the donut pan. Bake for 10 minutes. Turn the pan. Bake for another 10 minutes.
8. Remove from pan and let cool. Serve.

Day 5

Breakfast: Oatmeal Peaches
Lunch: Steak in Rosemary
Dinner: Pickled Cucumber Salad
Dessert: Cranberry Puddings

Breakfast

Oatmeal Peaches

Ingredients:
- 3 cups water
- 1 cup steel cut oats
- 1 tablespoon pure maple syrup
- 1 large ripe peach, chopped
- ¼ teaspoon vanilla extract
- ¼ teaspoon salt
- ¼ cup raw walnuts
- 1 tablespoon chia seeds

Directions:
1. Put 3 cups of water and oats into a saucepan. Let it simmer for 15 minutes. Stir occasionally until the oats have absorbed the water.
2. Add the maple syrup, peaches, vanilla extract, and salt. Stir well.
3. Pour the oatmeal into a bowl and sprinkle walnuts and chia seeds. Serve.

Lunch

Steak in Rosemary

Ingredients:
- 3 boneless beef loins
- 2 cloves garlic, minced

- 1 teaspoon lemon, grated
- 2 tablespoons rosemary leaves, minced
- 1 tablespoon extra-virgin olive oil
- 1 teaspoon black pepper
- Rosemary sprigs

Directions:

1. In a bowl, combine garlic, lemon, rosemary, oil, and pepper. Rub on the steaks. Marinade for 1 hour.
2. Grill steaks, medium rare. Cut into thick slices and garnish with rosemary sprigs. Serve.

Dinner

Pickled Cucumber Salad

Ingredients:

- 1 seedless cucumber, thinly sliced
- 1 shallot, thinly sliced
- ¼ cup rice wine vinegar
- 1 teaspoon sugar
- 1 small dill, minced
- ¼ teaspoon salt
- ¼ teaspoon pepper

Directions:

1. Put slices of cucumber and shallot in a salad bowl.

2. Add vinegar, sugar, dill, salt, and pepper.
3. Toss well and refrigerate for 20 minutes. Serve.

Dessert

Cranberry Puddings

Ingredients:
- 50g dried cranberries
- 50g dates, chopped
- 1 orange, zest and juice
- ½ teaspoon freshly ground nutmeg
- 75g brown sugar
- ¼ cup olive oil
- ½ cup applesauce
- Icing sugar

Directions:
1. Combine cranberries, dates, orange juice and zest, and nutmeg in a saucepan. Bring to a boil. Let cool and set aside.
2. Meanwhile, in another bowl, mix sugar and oil. Add the applesauce until combined well.
3. Grease a muffin tin and preheat the oven to 300 F. Pour pudding mixture over tins. Bake for 1 hour or until firm.
4. Remove and let cool for 15 minutes. Sprinkle with icing sugar. Serve.

Day 6

> Breakfast: Tomato and Spinach Frittata
> Lunch: Salmon Fillets Salad
> Dinner: Grilled Chicken in Red Pimiento Sauce
> Dessert: Leek and Cheese Quiche

Breakfast

Tomato and Spinach Frittata

Ingredients:

For the frittata

- 1 tablespoon olive oil
- 2 cloves garlic, minced
- 2 onions, sliced
- 1 package spinach
- 3 eggs
- 1/3 cup coconut milk
- ½ cup Tofutti cheese

For the Salsa

- 2 onions, minced
- 1 clove garlic, minced
- 4 tomatoes, chopped
- 2 tablespoons cilantro, minced
- 1 tablespoon lime juice
- ¼ teaspoon salt

- ⅛ teaspoon pepper

Directions:

1. Preheat the oven to 350 F. Heat the oil in a skillet.
2. For the frittata: Add garlic and onion. Cook for 3 minutes or until tender. Add the spinach.
3. Meanwhile, in a small bowl, beat the eggs and milk. Whisk until foamy.
4. Pour the egg mixture over spinach and cook for 8 minutes. Add some cheese. Bake for 10 minutes.
5. For the salsa: combine onions, garlic, tomatoes, cilantro, lime juice, salt, and pepper. Pour over the frittata. Serve.

Lunch

Salmon Fillets Salad

Ingredients:

For the salmon:

- 2 lbs wild caught salmon
- Pinch of salt
- 1 tablespoon olive oil

For the salad:

- 1 cucumber, thinly sliced
- 2 tablespoons rice wine vinegar
- 2 tablespoons Thai fish sauce
- 1 pineapple, thinly sliced

- ½ cup fresh mint
- 1 tablespoon lime juice
- 1 tablespoon raw honey

Directions:

1. For the salmon: rub sea salt on both sides. Let stand for 15 minutes until ready to cook.
2. Heat the oil. Cook the fish for 3 minutes skin-side down. Flip through the other side. Cook for another 3 minutes or until golden brown.
3. For the salad: mix together cucumber, vinegar, Thai fish sauce, pineapples, mint, lime juice, and honey.
4. Transfer salmon onto a platter and top with cucumber and pineapple salad.

Dinner

Grilled Chicken in Red Pimiento Sauce

Ingredients:

- 1 teaspoon dried oregano
- ½ teaspoon ground cumin
- ½ cup extra virgin olive oil
- ½ teaspoon ground cloves
- 3 cloves garlic, minced
- 5 boneless chicken breast
- Red pimento sauce

Directions:

1. In a large bowl, mix together oregano, cumin, oil, cloves, and garlic.
2. Add chicken breast and coat well.
3. Cook on a grill for 30 minutes.
4. Spread red pimiento sauce over cooked chicken. Serve.

Dessert

Leek and Cheese Quiche

Ingredients:

For the crust pastry

- 1 tablespoon olive oil
- 250g whole wheat flour
- Pinch of sugar
- Pinch of salt
- 2 eggs
- 1 tablespoon almond oil

For the filling

- 1 tablespoon olive oil
- 2 leeks, trimmed
- 1 teaspoon curry powder
- Pinch of salt
- Pinch of pepper
- 500 ml coconut cream

- 100g low-fat cheese

Directions:

For the pastry: Rub oil and flour together until a breadcrumb-like consistency is achieved. Add sugar and salt. Beat the eggs and pour over the mixture. Add almond oil to form a dough. Set aside for 2 hours.

1. Scatter flour on a tabletop. Even out pastry. Set aside for 1 hour.
2. Preheat the oven to 325 F. Coat pastry shell with greaseproof sheet. Blind bake for 20 minutes. Take off paper. Set aside tart shell.
3. In a saucepan, heat the oil. Put the leeks in. Season with curry powder, salt, and pepper. Remove from pan. Set aside.
4. In a bowl, put the coconut cream. Crumble the cheese.
5. Transfer leeks to the pastry shell and put the egg mixture in. Bake for 45 minutes. Serve warm.

Day 7

Breakfast: Spinach Breakfast Salad

Lunch: Green Onion, Chile and Avocado

Dinner: Eggplant Caviar

Dessert: Cheese Soufflé

Breakfast

Spinach Breakfast Salad

Ingredients:
- 2 teaspoons vegetable oil
- Dash of Worcestershire sauce
- 1 ½ teaspoons sugar
- 3 teaspoons balsamic vinegar
- 3 cups packed spinach
- ½ cup tomatoes
- 1 oz Tofutti cheese

Directions:
1. Combine oil, Worcestershire sauce, sugar, and vinegar in a bowl. Mix and set aside.
2. Put rinsed spinach in a bowl. Add tomatoes to the spinach.
3. Pour the dressing onto the tomatoes and spinach. Sprinkle with Tofutti cheese. Serve immediately.

Lunch

Green Onion, Chile and Avocado

Ingredients:
- 1 teaspoon olive oil
- ½ green chile, diced
- 1 tablespoon onion, minced
- 1 tablespoon cilantro
- 1 tablespoon cheddar cheese

- ½ ripe avocado, sliced

Directions:

1. In a skillet, heat the olive oil. Add chile and onion. Cook for 8 minutes.
2. Set aside and combine the cilantro.
3. Make the omelet. Add the chile-onion mixture. Put cheese and serve with avocadoes.

Dinner

Eggplant Caviar

Ingredients:
- 2 tablespoons olive oil
- 1 tablespoon cumin seeds
- 4 cloves garlic, minced
- 1 large eggplant
- ½ teaspoons peppercorns
- ½ cup tomatoes, diced
- 3 onions, chopped
- 1 red bell pepper, roasted
- 2 sun-dried tomatoes, chopped
- 1 ½ tablespoons red wine vinegar
- ½ cup parsley leaves, chopped
- Pinch of salt
- Pinch of pepper

Directions:

1. In a skillet, toast cumin seeds for 4 minutes. Put on a spice grinder and ground. Set aside.
2. In a skillet, add 1 tablespoon of oil. Add the eggplant in batches. Stir continuously until brown in color. Add cumin, garlic, peppercorns, and tomatoes. Cook for 1 hour.
3. Transfer to a blender and process until smooth. Mix together onions, roasted pepper, sun-dried tomatoes, vinegar, and parsley until well blended. Add salt and pepper, and then chill.

Dessert

Cheese Soufflé

Ingredients:

- 1 tablespoon olive oil
- 300ml almond milk
- 1 small onion, quartered
- 2 carrots, chopped
- 3 black peppercorns
- ½ cup thyme leaves
- ½ cup bay leaves
- ½ cup parsley stalks
- 50g whole grain flour
- 3 eggs
- 110g goat's cheese, crumbled
- 50g Parmesan cheese, finely grated

- Cayenne, freshly ground
- Pinch of salt
- Nutmeg

Directions:

1. Preheat the oven to 450 F.
2. In a saucepan, put milk, onion, carrots, peppercorns, thyme, bay leaves, and parsley. Bring to boil. Set aside.
3. Put oil and flour in another pan. Cook for 3 minutes. Whisk until it thickens. Let cool. Add the eggs, goat's cheese, and Parmesan cheese. Season with cayenne, salt, and nutmeg.
4. Spoon the mixture in a plate. Sprinkle on thyme leaves and the remaining Parmesan cheese. Bake in the oven for 20 minutes or until golden and puffed up. Serve.

Chapter 8 – The Daily Challenges and Workout Routines You Can Do

Many people fail in diet programs and the South Beach Diet is no exception. While many view it as an easy-to-follow diet program, some say that it is easy at the beginning and becomes more challenging as the days progress. This diet encourages followers to eat until they are not hungry, even on the more stringent phase of the first 2 weeks, provided that they munch on healthier eats.

Those who are trying to look for an effective diet program would normally find it easy to start just about any kind of program because it is human nature to be excited about a new diet, especially if it promises weight loss. You feel optimistic and motivated to get your health and physical looks back on track. You lose pounds and see fat melt away in just a short period of time. You begin digging out old clothes and finally can fit into your 10-year old dress or pants. Sticking with the program is a walk in the park as long as you see positive results. But what happens next?

In the South Beach Diet, the real challenge begins after you succeed in losing pounds during the first 2 weeks. At the time of transition from Phase One to Two, you will have definitely lost a lot of weight. As you begin to reintroduce fruits and other carbs into your diet, your weight loss begins to move at a slower pace. That can be disappointing to a dieter. Therefore, you decide to stay longer on Phase One. While some have managed to stay on Phase One for good, know that there will likely come a point when you will slide and fail.

And here are other reasons why dieters fail:

- You have to realize that Phase One is not forever. It is not meant for the long-term. You have stuck to steamed and grilled lean fish and meat, low-fat cheese, salads, and celery sticks. After some time, all these foods will get dull.

- Dieters, on their attempt to be on Phase One for a longer period of time than what is recommended, try devising and experimenting with different meal combinations. That is good, but how long can this go on for? Others even go as far as breaking the rules.

- Some would follow Phase One strictly for more than two weeks but they would cheat on a small cookie when hunger strikes, snack on some chips at night, and have a few sips of soda now and then. All considered together, that is cheating more than it is dieting.

- Sometimes, when dieters on Phase Two need to revert to Phase One, they no longer find it exciting. Everything becomes monotonous, and this impairs the dieters' discipline until they are eventually off track.

- Another reason why people fail is that their everyday chores and responsibilities get in the way. They often feel stressed-out, and in order for them to relieve stress, they would have a bite of some forbidden food.

What to do when you are in this situation?

First, you have to like what you eat. The menus and recipes provided in this eBook will help you be more aware of the kind of food to eat. If you will notice, the specified meals run only from Days 1-7. After that it is up to you to make combinations or add more recipes to your food plan.

Second, do not let stress get the better of you. Work-related stress is usually the main culprit. If you are stressed out at work, take a moment to breathe and relax. Think of it this way: you have come a long way with your diet regimen. Do not let a stressful day ruin everything.

Third, think of the South Beach Diet as your usual and everyday eating lifestyle. Consider this diet not as commands laid out in stone. Instead, think of it as part of your everyday life. Many people fail because their mindset is that they are "on a diet". If you keep your mind off dieting and just follow the South Beach Diet as naturally as a possible, you will see eating in a different light.

Finally, love your health and do your body a favor. Eat healthy so you can expect to live a healthier and fuller life.

The following are some of the common exercises that you can do as you follow the South Beach Diet. Remember, diet alone is not enough. You have to get moving.

Exercises for Everyday Weight Loss
Before you begin the exercise routines, you need to warm up those muscles to help prepare for the workout session. It is better that you begin familiarizing yourself with the following terminology:

1. Repetition – This is considered to be a complete move or pose. This would usually take about 9 seconds. That is four seconds to raise the weight if you are using weights, one second of pause, and four seconds to get back to the starting pose.

2. Set – This is the number of repetitions in each exercise. Each move would usually make for eight repetitions. And, two sets are done for each routine.

3. Rest – This is done between sets. It usually takes a minute in order to prepare the body for the next move.

Warm Up Exercises

Stretch

This will help prevent injury and will contribute to your flexibility. If you are doing strength training, it is best that you begin with aerobics and then stretch train. You can save a good stretch for the end of a vigorous exercise session. The basic instructions for stretching are simple: first, you need to get into the position, extend your muscles as far as you can, and hold the position for 20 seconds. Remember to breathe as normally as possible.

During the stretch, try to extend the position but never go to the point of discomfort. Relax the muscles and do not overdo stretching.

Here are some examples of stretches:

1. The Shoulder Stretch – This particular routine stretches the muscles on the shoulders and upper arms.

How to do it:

- Stand with feet shoulder-width apart and the arms at the sides.

- Extend the arms straight behind the body and pull the arms back as high as you can.

- Clasp your hands together if you can.

2. The Quadriceps Stretch – This is done standing up with a chair in front of you for support.

How to do it:

- Hold onto a chair with your left hand and bend your right knee so the left leg comes up behind you.

- Grasp the ankle and hold it. Point the knee down. Hold this position for 20 seconds and then release. Switch to the other side.

- Remember: do not force yourself if you cannot reach your ankle especially when you bend your knee and raise your leg behind you. If you find it uncomfortable, you can just bend your knee and lower your leg back down.

3. The Lower Leg Stretch – This particular routine stretches the legs and ankles.

How to do it:

- Sit in a chair with feet flat on the floor. Extend the legs slightly so the heels are one to two inches off the floor.

- Flex toes up and bend ankles back towards you.

- Hold the stretch for 20 seconds. Then point the toes down, and your feet away from you as far as possible. Hold the stretch for 20 seconds.

4. The Lower Back Stretch – This stretches the back muscles as well as the hamstrings.

How to do it:

- Sit forward in a chair with feet flat on the floor. The lower legs and thigh should form a right angle. Slide the left leg forward whilst keeping the heel on the floor or until the right knee is straight. The ankle must be in a relaxed position.

- Extend both arms and point the fingers toward the right foot. Bend your right foot as far as you can reach and as comfortable as you can.

- Hold the position for 20 seconds and then release. Repeat and switch sides.

If you are stuck at home, do not worry. The truth is, you do not need to go to the gym in order to lose weight while on a South Beach Diet. Try the following exercises:

1. Overhead Press – This exercise specifically targets the shoulders and arms. If you have unsightly fats in your arms, this exercise will help you with your "batwings" or the fat you see at the back of your upper arm.

How to do it:

- Starting position: Stand straight shoulder-width apart. Place dumbbells on each hand.
- Hold the dumbbells with the palms facing forward.
- Push dumbbells up until the arms are over the head. Put the dumbbells a little to your front.
- Slowly lower the weights and go back to starting position.

2. Pelvic tilt – This exercise strengthens your midsection – the abdomen, thighs, back, and buttocks. This is considered a perfect complement to a basic weight loss program. This is easy to do and all you need is a firm mattress.

How to do it:

- Lie on your back with knees bent and both feet flat on the ground.
- The arms should be relaxed and at your sides with the palms flat on the floor.
- Slowly roll up your pelvis off the floor. This can be done by lifting first the hips, waist, and the lower back. The midsection must form a straight line from the knees

to the upper back. The shoulders should remain grounded on the floor. Pause for breath.

3. Front Leg Raise – This is an ideal thigh-shaper. This exercise strengthens the legs and helps with strenuous physical activities such as jogging, brisk walking, and even rising up from a chair.

How to do it:

- Sit on the floor with your back leaning backwards slightly. Put both hands behind the buttocks to support the upper body.

- Extend the legs straight in front of you. The left knee should be bent with the left foot on the floor next to the right leg and above the ankle.

- Slowly lift the right leg as high as you can. Keep it straight with toes pointing up and the foot relaxed. Pause for breath and then slowly lower down to the floor.

4. Chair Stand – This exercise targets the thighs, abdominals, and buttocks. It also helps you improve your balance and is considered a perfect warm up exercise.

How to do it:

- Sit facing the chair with feet flat on the ground. In a cross arm position, hold them against the chest. The fingertips must touch the shoulders.
- Slightly lean forward not forgetting to keep your back straight. Then, stand up. Your weight must come from the legs and buttock muscles.
- Go back to the starting position. Pause for breath and then repeat.

5. Reverse Chair Stand – In this kind of exercise, your success will depend on moving slowly. You must use your buttock muscles and legs in order to lower yourself. Should this be a challenging one for you, you may use both hands for support.

How to do it:

- Start by practicing sitting down and standing up without hand support. Just make sure that when you do so, you are going to land on the chair safely.
- Stand in front of the chair with feet shoulder-width apart and your head held high.
- Both arms must be extended and form a straight line with palms facing down and parallel to the ground.
- Slowly bend the hips while the back is straight. Aim the buttocks backwards as you lean forward.
- Pause for breath and then raise yourself up to repeat.

Aerobics

Along with strength training, it is also important that you have Plan B should Plan A not work. While you are on the South Beach Diet, make it a habit to give yourself some good exercise such as aerobics.

The following are basic measures to take note of in order to make your aerobics sessions successful and more enjoyable:

The Dress Code

To make your workout pleasurable, you must dress comfortably. While some get inspiration from stylish exercise gear, know that keeping it simple is just fine.

Some of the most important factors include:

- Dressing for safety – Wear an outfit that won't get caught in moving equipment. If you plan to jog at night, wear clothes that have reflective strips. If you are going out cycling, wear a helmet. Safety must be your primary consideration.
- Select a type of shoes that fit well. Good athletics shoes are worth buying. Picking the right shoes eliminates the possibility of injuries during exercise.

Exercise Equipment
It is also important that you check the equipment before buying or using it. Look for safety notices and recommended usage instructions. Do not experiment, especially if the equipment is unfamiliar and you are going to use it for the first time. Give it a good look and make sure it is in perfect condition. Otherwise, seek the assistance of a well-trained professional. Or if you are at home, read the user's manual.

Choose a Safe Place to Work Out
If you are going outdoors to exercise, take sensible precautions. Do not exercise during the morning rush or in dangerous traffic. Take note of unsafe neighborhoods and be mindful of the people you come across on the streets. An exercise buddy is all the more helpful in ensuring your personal safety.

Drink Plenty of Water
Just as when you are dieting, it is important to keep yourself hydrated during exercise. The body requires water during physical activity. When you perspire, you keep the body cool and release additional moisture through respiration. This is one of the reasons why it is important to drink plenty of water. And, to ensure that you are getting enough, drink at least a cup of water before working out.

Drink another cup within 45 minutes after exercising. If an activity is prolonged or you are going hiking, drink water every hour.

How do you monitor hydration? Look at your urine and examine it. The normal color range is pale yellow to almost clear. If it is dark, then that is your body telling you that you are dehydrated.

Limit distractions
In order to make for an effective workout, make sure that distractions are limited. Exercise is enjoyable but do not let petty interruptions get in the way. Focus on what you are doing, feel your body move, and your muscles stretch.

Measure the heart rate
You can either buy heart rate monitors at sports centers or you can monitor your heart rate manually. This can be done by taking your radial pulse.

To take a radial pulse, you need a watch with a second hand.

- First, bend your right arm at the elbow and hold the right hand out.
- Hold the forefinger and middle finger of your left hand together. Touch them to the base of your right thumb.
- Slide the fingers across the wrist and move them to the top of the right arm. The left fingers should cross the bones of the right wrist. From there, you will feel a hollow located in the right forearm between the tendons and bone on top.
- Press firmly when you have reached the hollow part. You should feel the radial pulse there. If not, you can try bending the right wrist slightly.
- As you feel your pulse, look at your watch and count the number of beats for 15 seconds.

Your Workout Plan

Just as you have a South Beach Diet plan, you must also have a fitness plan. They say that the easiest way to develop a habit of physical activity is to choose the kind that is readily available at your disposal. If you love going outdoors for exercise, you can go jogging, hiking, or biking. If you are a homebody, you can use the treadmill, exercise bike, and perform some aerobic exercises.

To help you decide which exercise you wil do, this eBook will give you some of the most popular exercises meant for beginners. You can pick whichever one suits your lifestyle. Remember, as long as you get those muscles working, anything that allows you to workout at the right intensity is considered good.

Walking
This is considered to be the most ideal workout routine, and that is for good reason. When you walk, your cardiovascular system also gets a workout. It is through walking that you are able to tone your legs and it's also good if you are trying to lose weight. Walking burns fat fast and there is no equipment needed, so it is easy to do. Another added convenience of walking is that it can be a part of your everyday routine such as running errands or traveling by foot.

When you walk, observing good posture is a must. And as you do so, it is also important that you increase the intensity. One way to do this is to walk faster, do a brisk walk, or do a combination of both jogging and running.

Most people who exercise by walking increase the intensity by carrying weights when they walk. But that is not recommended to do regularly. Adding weight as you walk briskly could impair your balance and lead to joint injuries.

For those who would rather walk indoors, you can use a treadmill. You can use either a manual or an electric one. Look for a treadmill that is adjustable, with a wide belt, and that is steady when you walk. Also, you need to ensure that the surface is long enough for strides. When you use a treadmill, it is suggested that you hold on to the handrail until you get the hang of it and feel comfortable at your chosen pace. But as soon as you can manage without holding on to the handrails, feel free to swing your arms as you stride. This will help you burn more calories.

Rowing
There is specific equipment meant for this workout routine. Rowing works the upper and lower body, particularly the abdominals. Plus, it does not strain the joints.

When you begin rowing, make sure that you check the oars. This is the bar that you pull back. The resistance and the stroke rate need not be high in order to achieve a good workout. There are two parts for each stroke. One, you pull the oars toward your body and stretch your legs as you do so. Just don't lock your knees as you row. Second, stretch your arms forward and then bend your knees. Remember, the arms need to go past the knees before they bend.

Cycling
This is also considered an excellent cardiovascular workout. By just pedaling, you burn calories faster and work the muscles in the upper body area. If you want to tone your abs and achieve firmer buttocks, you should consider cycling.

Cycling is easy on the joints, plus you need not feel bored when you do this cycle since you can either see nice scenery on a real bicycle or enjoy some TV on a stationary bicycle.

Stationary cycles (a.k.a. exercise bikes) come in different forms. There is the semi-recumbent with a back, and the upright type which is similar to a regular bicycle. Most cycles only train the lower body, but some equipment includes an arm that also works out the upper body. When you go to the gym, there are stationary cycling lessons. They include a series of movements involving the arms and shoulders as you pedal.

If you wanted to buy one for your home gym, choose handlebars that are comfortable and are just the right distance in front. Choose the one that will not make your arms fully stretched out or cramped. Also, you need to pick one that can easily be adjusted, especially the seat and the height.

When you get onto the stationary bike, feel the seat and make sure you are comfortable. Experiment by tilting slightly, pedaling, and doing arm movements until you find a comfortable position. Finally, make sure that you set the resistance. The recommended resistance that you should pedal is between 55 to 65 revolutions per minute.

Stair Climbing
This is another excellent cardiovascular workout that you will find easy to do with the correct equipment. It is akin to climbing up staircases. Those who like exercising outdoors do stair climbing by doing it at outdoor stadiums. This is popular among athletes as it helps condition the legs, thighs, calves, abdomen, and the back. However, if you have knee issues or injuries, you can still try stair climbing but opt for the semi-recumbent type. This supports the entire body weight and is definitely easier than its counterpart.

For those who are working out indoors, purchasing a machine is ideal. You can select a model that has smooth stepping action. Particularly pay attention to the foot plates: make sure that they are sturdy enough and won't cause you to slip.

Good posture is also important. Stand tall and do not slouch. Do not lean on the handrails. Straighten up and do a stair-climb motion.

Swimming

This is another calorie burner. Aside from the workout it provides, it also trains the upper and lower body. Through swimming, you can learn different strokes and be able to vary your routine for added intensity. However, it is a little difficult to gauge the intensity if you are swimming in the water since you are not sweating. The best thing to do is to take your pulse. Remember the radial pulse discussed? Go over the steps once again and practice taking your pulse.

Chapter 9 – Common Questions about the South Beach Diet and Your Exercise Program

When you are working towards a specific goal, you will go all the way and pour your heart into it. That is a common way of helping yourself keep on track. In the South Beach Diet, you have learned that it is important that you follow Phases One, Two, and Three. But since this diet is designed to be simple, failing should not demotivate you. Instead, pick up where you left off and start over again. The same goes for your designed exercise program. You should not feel demotivated when you fail to do your exercise. Instead, make this your motivation to exercise even harder.

Is it okay to weigh your progress?

Definitely. Almost all diets encourage stepping onto the weighing scale for progress. Aside from the added motivation, your weight can vary two or three pounds in a day due to the differences in the amount of water that you take in on a daily basis. However, these are but normal variations. So to weigh or not to weigh? Yes, you should weigh your progress and write it down in your weight goal journal.

How about body composition measurements?

This is often done with the use of a tape measure or those that claim to measure body fats. But know that most of the time, they are not accurate. The most accurate way to know if you have lost body fat is to measure yourself if you think you have a lost significant amount of pounds. In the South Beach Diet, you are expected to lose weight of about 8-13 pounds in two weeks. If you measure below the target pounds, you will find it hard to see any difference.

Should I have better medical results after the South Beach Diet?

Many South Beach Dieters who have managed to lose weight safely through this diet program can attest to better medical results. One of the most satisfying changes is that you can have improved health. Your blood sugar, blood pressure, and blood cholesterol will surprisingly be at a normal level as compared to before. Now that is the kind of improvement that you should aim for, besides looking good!

Am I eating more than I realize?

When you are following a specific diet plan, it is a bit tricky to know if you are really eating right. If you think you are losing weight and are religiously following the three Phases, there is nothing to worry about. But, if you have failed to adhere in the second week, don't fret. You can always go back to the start. There is really nothing wrong with that just as long as you know at what point you gave in to your cravings and are able to correct them.

Am I exercising at the right intensity?

If you are doing cardiovascular exercises, you should be able to increase the intensity of your chosen exercises within two to three weeks. When it comes to strength training, you should be able to lift heavier weights than usual.

If you are not seeing any changes at all and you still feel that your endurance does not take you to the next level, you might need to push yourself a bit harder. Your workout should make you sweat a lot. This will help in burning those calories and continuously burn more even if you have stopped working out. If you are still on a plateau – something that should be impossible on the South Beach Diet – set an appointment with your doctor. There might be some underlying health issues you must first attend to before you continue with said diet program.

Are you drinking enough water?

It is said over and over again that a person needs a total of eight glasses of water in a day, especially during the hot season. Failure to do so will result in dehydration. Also, you must be very careful not to mistake thirst for hunger. When you feel hungry, try drinking water first before eating again. This will help you gauge whether you are really hungry or just plain thirsty.

Are you under stress?

Most dieters fail because they are under stress. Pressures, whether at home or at the office, could eat away your energy. But how do you combat stress when you are on a diet? Just think of the outcome and the long term benefits of the South Beach Diet in your health and life as a whole. If you focus on the positive, it should be easier to escape the feeling of being stressed out.

Am I really losing weight?

Sometimes, weight loss stops the moment you still feel heavier than you want to be. You try following the South Beach Diet and the menus in this eBook but still feel heavy. The first thing you can do is to weigh and measure yourself. It is impossible not to lose weight when you cut out the bad carbs altogether for 2 weeks. So before you believe that you are not losing weight, check your vital statistics.

If you find it hard to follow the three Phases here, the situation calls for reassessment of your weight loss goals. The most important thing is that you ask yourself whether you are ready for the South Beach Diet. Determine if you really are because if you are half-hearted, no matter how promising the diet plan is, you will still fail. But if you are determined to reach your desired weight and have committed to follow this diet plan, then you must do everything in your power to keep your goals on track.

Is listening to your appetite important?

During the weeks of weight loss, you have eaten slightly less than your usual food intake, and good food at that. This has required you to tame your natural appetite. And therafter, it has to perform its natural task of regulating food intake so it matches with your energy expenditure. This is the reason why you only do Phase One for 2 weeks. You can't be there for too long. Armed with ample information, learn what hunger feels like and know how to properly respond to it. With continuing success, you will surely lose weight and reap the rewards of good health.

Is the South Beach Diet for me?

The South Beach Diet is for everyone. This diet is for those who want to lose weight but do not want a complicated food plan. This diet is for those who want to gain control of their cravings and finally make heathier choices in their everyday life. Finally, this diet is for those who want to be in the pink of health, combat heart disease, and the onset of diabetes. If you are planning to follow this diet regimen, now is the perfect time to do so. This eBook is your guide to what you need to know about the South Beach Diet. Do not be left behind. Be more beautiful inside and out.

Printed in Great Britain
by Amazon